## What readers are saying...

*"I found this book to be a page turner. As the author reviews her life story, I found myself reviewing mine...although in a totally different way than I have ever done before....Marybeth gently, but expertly, guides the reader to find the joy in even the most difficult times in our lives. She helps us to understand that by completing this exercise day by day, moment by moment...we are creating a blueprint of how to move forward to live our most authentic life."*

—Andrea Parkhill, RN BSN

*"This book was inspiring in so many ways. The author had a way of sharing from her own wealth of wisdom, experience and heartbreak. Her encouraging spirit carries through each word and encouraged me, the reader. I not only felt better for reading this book, but also recommended it to others who are on a journey to joy."*

—Esther Hughes, author, speaker, entrepreneur, and communications mentor to women. *Take 21, The Difference A Day Can Make*, and *Psalms and Prayers for People Affected by Cancer*

*"Marybeth has developed an easy transformational process to guide you to the life you've dreamed of. Marybeth knows loss! Her heartfelt book is your inspirational guide to creating a life you can love again. You are not alone! This inspirational book is exactly what you've been looking for—start your confident joy filled life now!"*

—Carol Walkner, energy healer, psychic medium, author, *Getting There From Here: Creative Strategies to Transform Your Business & Life*

# How to Soar
# with a Broken Wing

*Finding Tiny Moments
of Joy Every Day*

Marybeth Gregg

*To Suzanne,*
*Thank you for your friendship, love and*
*wisdom. Wishing you Joy, everyday.*
*With love,*
*Marybeth*

MIND*SHIFT*
Publishing

Sea Girt, New Jersey

*July 20, 2022*

Mindshift Publishing
P. O. Box 70
Sea Girt, New Jersey 08750
www.ticwl.com

ISBN 979-8-9854507-0-5  print
ISBN 979-8-9854507-1-2  e-book

Cover Design: Susan Beth Jones  sbestdesigns.com
Book Design: Anita Jones  anotherjones.com

Publisher's Cataloging-In-Publication Data
(Prepared by The Donohue Group, Inc.)

Names: Gregg, Marybeth, author,

Title: How to soar with a broken wing : finding tiny moments of joy every day / Marybeth Gregg.

Description: Sea Girt, New Jersey : Mindshift Publishing, [2022] | Includes bibliographical references.

Identifiers: ISBN 9798985450705 (softcover) | ISBN 9798985450712 (ebook)

Subjects: LCSH: Joy. | Attitude (Psychology) | Change (Psychology) | Stress management. | Work-life balance. | LCGFT: Self-help publications.

Classification: LCC BF575.H27 .G74 2022 (print) | LCC BF575.H27 (ebook) | DDC 158.1--dc23

Printed in the United States of America

*"One can never consent to creep
when one feels an impulse to soar."*

**—Helen Keller**

# Dedication

To my parents, Dorothy and George, who gave me unconditional love every day.

In loving memory of my husband, Harry, who loved me every moment and who surrounded me with Joy and Laughter. You encouraged me to be the best I could be and showed me how laughter and kindness could get us through anything. I miss you every day.

To my beautiful and loving daughter Sarah, who is the light of my life, you truly bring great joy to my life every day.

# Table of Contents

# The Beginning

Although this is my story, you will find that within, some of it is your story as well. It is written for you—for women who are on their own journey and perhaps are a bit lost or unsure of what to do next, or of who they really are. This book is for women who want to know how to get more control over their lives and find more joy within. This last year, and now, are unprecedented times of uncertainty, but what I know for certain is so many things are not working anymore! We all need some gentle and powerful guidance to not only "get through," but flourish and become who we need to be.

I thank you for reading this book, and I appreciate and admire you for wanting to be happier, for getting out of your comfort zone, and for taking this step to bring more joy into your life.

As our lives unfold, we learn that we receive both joy and pain, profound sorrows and deep moments of happiness, as if we were walking on air. It is a cycle, but sometimes we become stuck in the depths of sorrow and it can be nearly impossible to see our way out. I have learned that in those times, there are gifts we can open every day—tiny moments of joy to see us through the dark, teaching us how to make room for the light all around us.

Discovering this all started with my journey...

Marybeth Gregg

# Introduction

# My Journey – Your Invitation

My life began behind the backdrop of the rolling green farms of the idyllic Dutch country that populated so much of southeastern Pennsylvania. To see Amish families bringing fresh vegetables to market was a very common occurrence, and my dad always took such care to avoid driving our big Pontiac (and it was always a Pontiac) too close to the lumbering horse and buggies that would slowly make their way along the edge of the road. We lived in a very small city in the middle of this farmland, but it was a friendly, slow-paced life filled with dozens of cousins and friends, hours of playing outdoors, and days of school and church and family gathering. There were always simple family meals made from food fresh from the Farmer's Markets…a tiny moment of joy each day.

The truth is, I did have a special upbringing.

I had a mother and a father who worked together as a true team. They were quiet people, second-generation Americans, who both worked hard but never allowed themselves to become dominated by the stresses of their work. They were the helpers at church and school. They made time each day for family and for each other.

I was an only child, but I never felt lonely with the tribe of twenty-some cousins always around, the playmates everywhere, and the scores of aunts and uncles in the neighborhood. We sat on porches

1

or on the stoops and watched everyone walk by. That was enough for us. We were entertained. We were happy.

With my parents, there were no gender roles assigned, no war of the sexes, no bitter arguments and resentments, just a happy and productive partnership and a warm and loving environment.

I remember my mother and father dancing to the Big Band tunes on the radio. Dancing in the kitchen. Dancing in the living room. Dancing in the dining room. Every day. Their tiny moments of joy.

I remember joining in with them sometimes. I remember laughing.

I remember trips across the country in my father's beloved Pontiac. I remember Broadway plays in New York City. I remember the overflowing excitement of getting on the train (when they were still running) to go on a shopping trip to the big Wanamakers in Philadelphia. As a little girl, I would look up with wonder, and ride the wood-paneled elevators as the operator asked politely if I would like to go to the floor with the girl's dresses. You bet I did!

I remember my many cousins running about and playing with me daily. We would climb trees, draw hop scotch in the alley, play hide and seek until it got dark or we were called in for dinner. One would have never known that I was an only child.

I remember working diligently at school and I remember the community we formed together at church. Especially during Lent, when services would go on so long that we would come out with our knees red. That had a way of bringing people together.

I remember heavenly meals and learning about the value of good, nourishing food early on. I would watch as grapes were loaded straight off the curb in the fall for wine-making, and as scores of mouth-watering foods were unloaded at the local Farmer's Market where the Amish would cart only their freshest vegetables, meats, and perfectly baked sticky buns. It was the original farm to table.

I remember streets that were safe enough to play in until sundown, when we could race home for a dinner of spaghetti and meatballs, or roast beef with gravy and mounds of whipped potatoes. I remember peaceful nights fueled by the kind of beautiful tiredness that can only come after long days of playing outside and catching lightning bugs in a glass jar—always making sure we punched holes in the lid so they could breathe. They lit our small hands and we were in wonder.

Life was its own kind of heaven.

As I look back at it now, it sure seems like it was all too good to be true. After a life of coaching women through harrowing experiences and hearing story after story of painful childhoods, horrific abuse, and negligent parenting, how could I be so different? Did I just draw some magic lot in life? Was this real?

The truth is, it was real. However, it wouldn't be my life forever. My struggles and pain arrived later. We all take our turn—our moments of joy, our moments of sorrow. Somehow, what we learn about years of living and reliving the cycle is that the joy is there again if we only look for it.

In our world today, millions of women are wandering through life plagued by disappointments, heartaches, and a sense of impending dread that they have missed the boat on their great adventure and now it's too late to hop aboard. So many are saddled with deep pains as they are burdened by a crushing sense that their lives are not their own—their boat strayed off course and now they simply do not know where they are or where they are going.

Despite my beautiful childhood, my loving parents, and all the blessings this world has given me, I too found myself in the middle chapters of my life burdened by a continuous feeling that my destiny was not my own. Events happened in my life that made me feel as if I were spiraling out of control, that perhaps I was paying back for that beautiful childhood with some true tragedies in the later portion of my adult life. Some days I carried with me a sense that there were strong powers at work making it impossible for me to reshape my destiny and manifest the life I wanted. Now I am learning that all of these powers and messages are here for me to learn and thrive and grow.

I now know that these experiences were given to me for a reason, which I am still uncovering to this day. I know that by dedicating my days to making conscious choices, I have started to overcome, inch by inch, the disappointments and struggles of my life and understand that we get to have a cycle of Life Death Life again, without which we would be flat and unfulfilled. I am learning to embrace change and learn from it, always reminding myself that happiness and sorrow will come and go.

> *"Let everything happen to you: beauty and terror.*
> *Just keep going. No feeling is final."*
> **—Rainer Maria Rilke**

I wish I could tell you that throughout my journey I found what I was seeking, that I suddenly became "whole." However, I have embraced that it is the journey, and not just the goal, where life truly unfolds and presents us with unlimited gifts. What I can say is that I am working on myself every day. That joy has returned, sometimes in smaller bites, but I can breathe and smile again, and I feel blessed each day.

You are brilliantly capable of doing the same.

Struggles, big ones and small ones, will always come and go. They are a part of the natural rhythm of our lives. We fluctuate between comedy and tragedy, with the majority of life feeling like it's landing in some messy place in between.

We are equipped with choices. There will always be choices, and there will always be a way out of our struggles. Pain will always be present too, but that pain does not have to define us.

As we grow, we learn to honor our pain, our sorrows, our grief, and our loss. We train ourselves to stay with these sensations, to invite them into our homes and inevitably transcend them. These emotional cuts and bruises are telling us a story, and it's a very important one.

They tell us why we are here and what we are supposed to be. They tell us that we deserve change and we deserve happiness. They tell us that our life, when painted by courageous choices that are truly awake, can belong to us. We are in control of who we are, what we feel, and how we decide to address our pain.

Most important of all, our pain shows us that we have a deep reservoir of resilience within ourselves. Sometimes we may need some support, a guide to bring out that well, but it is within each and every one of us. I know it is. I know it in every fiber of my being.

We want the daily existence of our lives to be easy, but that is not how we learn and grow. Before we find a sense of peace, we have to accept and rise above some dark and difficult truths. We have to work on "letting go," so that we may open up room for the good things to come in.

There is a reverse side of this pain and difficulty. An easy choice, one that we can make with so much simplicity. Every day, thousands of tiny moments of joy are swirling around us.

**Small blessings are everywhere, populating our world and waiting to be captured. It is up to us to see them.**

I was taught this lesson growing up; it was almost encoded into my DNA. It was fundamental to my upbringing and the world that made me the woman I am today. It just took me time to cut through the levels of pain and disappointments that were clouding my ability to see the joy surrounding me, but it was always there.

As a modern woman, you are living in a world with rules and systems that are designed to hold you down, that want to see you ignored and want to keep things exactly the way they are now.

You will be spoken over; you will be belittled.

You will be told to live your life within the confines of a small bubble that you may never exceed the bounds of.

You will be called a little girl.

You will be called a bitch or worse.

You also may be called an old lady.

You will be asked to play your life on the small screen.

But you are not here to listen to all of that.

**You cannot let other people define you.**

You can and you must live your life large. That is how you will allow yourself to once again see the joy around you.

**We are a beautiful tribe of troublemakers.**

We are creative, we are chaotic, and we have an endless store of potential that is screaming to be released. The world is afraid of that release, but for you to be happy, you must jump in and make trouble; be what your heart tells you to be and do.

I am here to tell you that with our strongest inner conviction, we must trust in God, in a Universal Spirit, with a relentless focus on joy centered around becoming our best every day. Only then can we change our lives and the lives of others.

To be honest with you, I am still on my path toward getting to this place of joy and trust. I have come to a point in my life where I can finally say that I am living my life more fully, more awake, and in harmony with my pain and loss, but it is a journey I know will never end. It is a process that gets me a little closer each day to finding peace. The paradox of it all is, by accepting that we will never reach the end of this journey, true peace arrives.

So, I want to share with you my story so far. I want you to come with me on a journey of self-discovery, of pain and loss, and of unbreakable spirit so that you may find your own power within yourself and create the life that you deserve. My journey is only one amongst a large web of stories of women finding themselves amongst the pains and sorrows of our modern life.

What we all share in common is that along the way, we have all taken our own path to discovering and realizing these tiny moments of joy. They are there waiting for you as well.

I invite you now to share in my journey so that you may find little pieces of wisdom and learning to guide you along the way to your new path to joy. As you travel, I hope these stories will help you realize the most important message of all: you are not alone. There is a tribe of beautiful women all around, including myself, to support and inspire you at every turn of the road.

In this book, after each chapter, I have included Take Time Now to Reflect, because this book is for you—to reflect, to learn to laugh, to grow in your own unique and wonderful way. You may not be able to answer all the questions at this point. If you can't, just jot down the first thing you feel. I didn't say think—I said feel. Feelings are what truly speak to us and reflect what our heart wants us to hear.

Without further ado, let's begin.

# Chapter 1

*Playing Small*

One day while reading *Daring Greatly: How the Courage to Be Vulnerable Transforms the Way We Live, Love, Parent, and Lead* by one of my favorite authors, Brené Brown, I remembered being told about how children have to be quiet. Brené talks about the issue of women still staying "small, sweet, quiet, and modest," even though people believe it is no longer an issue. Many times, it is still here with us when women do speak up.

I remember how this started in my life. I can hear the usual refrain now, and perhaps you can as well.

*"Children are meant to be seen and not heard."*

If you were of a certain age, this was not a phrase; it was a gospel. For me, this clear expectation quickly transformed into hard lessons...very hard lessons.

In my town, most people knew their place. We had a very structured society, but I would not say that these rules were strictly enforced. There was no reason for them to be, because everyone naturally followed them.

This is simply what people did; this is how we behaved and how we lived. There was no back talking, there was no sass, there was no questioning of authority, and this way of life did not bother me at the time of my childhood. It was a source of comfort, a safe way of being. Who really wanted to color outside the lines? The picture was far prettier if we stayed within our structured bounds.

The result of all this? Looking back, I ended up living a small life.

To be clear, I lived a good life, a peaceful life, and a life full of support and love. Yet, it was a small life, in the sense that I was a follower rather than a designer of my own future.

The humor of it all is when I was young, this life seemed great. It was perfect for me at the time.

One day, I had to grow up. And what do you think I wanted?

I wanted a bigger life. A life where I was the writer of my own destiny, where my failures were squarely mine and so were my successes, my heartbreaks, my loves, and my joys.

As I matured and moved through my college career and early jobs, the tension between my small life and my desire for a larger one became an almost insurmountable conflict for me. In many ways, I thought the same ways as I did as a child; I kept my head down, I got the work done, and I didn't ask many questions. I was a good girl.

All along, I thought this was the right way. If I just stayed dedicated to the path I was on, somebody was bound to see all this diligence and hard work, right? I turned in every paper on time, expecting a cookie in return. Soon enough, I found there was not always going to be a cookie.

Looking back on my life, I see that this pattern of behavior was holding me back from vast potential. I had been trained from an early age to listen and to do. I was never taught to open up and create.

I would soon learn that creation is where our power lives.

We are not mindless robots; we are not simply obedient doers. We are makers. The process of creation is a spiritual process, and it is within this process where our power truly rests. Unfortunately, becoming a "maker" or a "creative" is something that has been discouraged for us as women for such a long time. It's too dangerous to have women running around with all that creativity. What if they broke down the established order? What if everything changed? What if there was chaos?

After a lifetime of spiritual growth, I have learned that chaos is a beautiful thing. Chaos is the source of our power. It is something we must embrace if we want to grow and learn. Chaos is the heartbeat of creativity, and I encourage you now—no matter what age you are—to bring chaos into your life. It is the first step to building that big life you've always dreamed of.

Structure keeps us docile. It keeps us small and it keeps us slaving away, so we don't have the time or the energy to ever question our place in the world. Chaos, on the other hand, lets us live freely. It lets us embrace our naturally inquisitive mind; it builds roads to new potential; it fills us with a beautiful, peaceful power that once released can never be squashed again.

If you want to stop living a small life, my first piece of advice is, paradoxically, to start small. What if you left your desk messy today? What if the clutter was no longer a problem, but a source of chaos and creativity? What if it was inspiration?

What would happen if you chose mindfully to no longer remain quiet, to ignore the household chores and the expectations to stay on the hamster wheel of doing more, more, more. What if you didn't make the bed every day? What if you had two pieces of chocolate because that's what you really, honestly wanted? Would the world burn down? Would society fall apart?

I hardly think so!

Throughout my time as a coach, I have worked with countless women CEOs, entrepreneurs, artists, and executives who all seem to struggle with one shared constraint: no matter how successful they have become, they still find themselves constantly questioning their skills, their worth, and their own personal identity.

I have found over time that the belief these women hold for themselves is so fragile that a simple flick of my finger could topple it over.

I specifically remember one client, a well-renowned and successful vice president of a major global company. At first glance, she seemed like she was sitting on the top of the world.

However, there was a darker underside to her success.

In work meetings, she had a reputation for wearing high-heeled shoes. During the heat of the discussion, she would quietly smile, look at you, and then throw those high heels against the wall—all to make a point. Colleagues and employees were terrified of her; business associates would approach her with extreme caution. Her leadership at this point came not from confidence but from control.

Eventually, we were able to connect during our sessions and make a breakthrough, mostly because I believe she did not view me as a threat to her power in the way she viewed many of her colleagues and fellow executives. She admitted to me that she believed this behavior stemmed from deep doubts hidden inside her. Despite the insurmountable level of control she displayed, she found herself riddled with insecurity and fear.

I found myself thinking, if a woman as powerful as her was plagued by so many doubts, how many other women out there are suffering just as silently? Women who may not be as successful, recognized, or articulate as this client.

I began to see that this was a larger problem for women, an infra-structural problem. No matter how high up the ladder we may ascend, self-doubt surrounds us everywhere. It holds us back from our potential, even when at first glance it may seem as if we are soaring. In reality, we are weighing ourselves down. We are letting the world and its expectations halt us from discovering our true potential. Worst of all, we are letting others force us into a life lived small.

We have been diligently, specifically, and consistently trained to live a small life. Somewhere along each of our paths, we became susceptible to the whims of the world and allowed ourselves to accept that smallness. As time went on, that belief festered inside of us, cementing into something permanent and stopping us from realizing the true extent of our potential.

As a result, our creativity has consequently gone dormant, and our power has shriveled into a shell of itself. Our sense of adventure has become neutralized and our tolerance of risk has become greatly reduced. We no longer take chances on who we could one day become. As a result, our potential shrinks and the possibilities of our life close. Stepping out of our comfort zone now equates to a feeling of pain, and we find ourselves trapped.

However, we are not stuck forever inside this future of living small. We can and must expand. It's easier than you would think.

There is a very famous quote from Marianne Williamson in *A Return to Love: Reflections on the Principles of "A Course in Miracles"* that is so profound. She asks, "Who am I to be brilliant, gorgeous, talented, fabulous?" This is a great question. According to Marianne, we cannot afford to be less than that! We are here to shine our brightest light on others, not our dimmest.

When we give ourselves the permission to slowly begin opening back up and shining our light again, we allow our creativity to take over. The effect will eventually begin compounding upon itself. The smallest taste of creativity and chaos will begin to spread...if you allow it.

Before you know it, your small doses of creativity will, step by step and bite by bite, turn into large storms of inspiration and power. You will find yourself enveloped by grand ideas and blessed with the energy and the drive to turn those grand ideas into grand practices. Before long, those grand practices will morph and cement into a grand life.

Step by step, you will turn a small life into a large life. And no one will be able to stop you.

### *How to Grab Tiny Moments of Joy*

I have learned that there are a few powerful things you can do to make sure you will grab those moments you need—the joy that is there for you. There are small things you can do every day that will help you acknowledge what is missing and help you build that fuller, bigger life you truly want.

- **Be aware of how you are *feeling*.** Is your energy low? Are you frustrated or snapping at others? Are you feeling taken for granted? Or any one of a hundred other emotions that are antithetical to your happy place and your best self? Awareness is the first step to beginning to take action.

- **Take three deep breaths.** This is a mandatory part for you to begin to find out what is not working. Close your eyes, step back, and slow down.

- **Have an honest conversation with yourself** about what is going on. Write it down in a journal, or keep an online journal.

- What are you doing that is putting you in a space that isn't ideal?

14

- What are you doing that brings a smile to your face?

Once you have these answers, you will start to see a pattern. For example, if you are working remotely and have seven hours of Zoom calls, ask yourself at the end of the day, do you feel productive or do you feel depleted? Make notes. Be introspective and honest about what moments brought a smile to your face! Keep taking notes and you will see the patterns I mentioned before.

If you are feeling depleted, indulge in a quick pick-me up. Take a walk around the block or in the park. Listen to the birds sing. This will do wonders for your mood, temperament, and energy.

### *Chapter 1 Summary*

The lesson of "children should be seen and not heard" has a negative effect on women as they enter adulthood. The adage teaches us to behave small, to live small...to be small.

This thought pattern will hold us back from living big and achieving the aspects of life we want most of all.

We are makers, not obedient robots. Society sees women taking hold of their creativity as a threat. Our creativity is a blessing to the world and accepting this is a necessary step to living large.

- Creativity is chaos, and chaos can be a beautiful thing. It can be a source of power and the antidote to an overly structured life that will only hold us down and keep us playing small.

- Living large paradoxically begins by starting small. What if I left my desk messy today? What if I ignore the household chores for a little while longer and write another chapter of my book? These small decisions work together to create a life lived large.

- No matter how high up the ladder we climb, due to our up-bringing, self-doubt will always find a way to creep in and stop women from reaching their full potential.

- Small doses of creativity will transform over time into large storms of inspiration and power.

### *Take Time Now to Reflect*

1. When were the times in your life when you felt you played small?

2. Why do you think that happened?

3. Do you know what you need to stop playing small now?

4. What does one Tiny Moment of Joy you create do to make you smile and laugh, and make your heart sing—if only for a few minutes?

# Chapter 2

## The Dutiful Me

I loved school, deeply.

Unlike many kids in elementary school, recess was not my favorite class—although I did love the fresh soft pretzels (a Pennsylvania thing) and running around screaming in the little concrete courtyard we had for a playground. The truth is, every class was my favorite class. Learning came easily to me. Education wasn't just important to me; it was deeply and truly enjoyable. My life seemed to revolve around the school day, but there was always time for fun. Weekends were filled with play and family dinners and doing everything outside until it got dark. And Mondays were anything but a drag; they were a great source of joy, because I got to learn. That is something that has stayed with me to this day.

While I had an instinct and a talent for learning and a deep hunger for education, I mostly loved school because there was a satisfaction in getting good grades, and I was doing what I was supposed to and received attention and praise. That's because I was such a sweet girl. And being a sweet girl meant teachers liked me and compliments were none too scare. I sought out good grades because good grades came with hard work, and it also meant I was not disappointing the nuns. I didn't want to disappoint anyone for the rest of my life.

This is not to say that I loved every minute of class; I wasn't a complete nut. Sitting through hours after hours of grammar class wasn't necessarily my idea of living my best life, but I never questioned it, because that was not something you did.

I spent so much time in class being bored over topics such as the all-important sentence declension, a subject I am fairly certain has lost all relevance in our current society. Back then, it was vital. Doing it according to the rules was the source of my identity and my supposed happiness.

Back then, I questioned nothing. I wrote multiplication tables over and over on the chalkboard until the chalk had been reduced to an unrecognizable stub. I burned lines of verse into my brain so that I would be properly prepared for the critical poetry reading session. I slammed my noses into those black and white marble notebooks and I wrote and wrote and wrote until the nun told me to stop.

I did everything I was told. And never once in my wildest imagination did I approach the thought of questioning authority. That was the dutiful me.

Every once in a blue moon, though, I would act out— silently. One of the sneaky things I would do was take a big grey felt eraser covered with chalk and wipe on the back of the nun's habit. Bad me! Of course, I never got caught.

Now, I look back at that time with so much confusion. I remember these moments with a sense of idyllic peace because emotionally this life was so joyous. I was truly and authentically happy in this system.

Though I did feel a sense of accomplishment when I was praised, I do not think this reaction came from a place of superiority over my fellow classmates. Ultimately, I believe I had been groomed in such a way that I had no choice but to follow everything I was told. Rebelling simply was not an option (until I made it to college and the inevitable wild woman stage occurred). At this point, why would I risk doing anything other than what was expected? Not only was that unacceptable; it brought about fear and a loss of safety.

That sense of fear ultimately held me back with a great degree of severity, a fact I would not realize until later in life.

In 1983, after a difficult divorce from my first husband, I decided to go on a Windjammer Cruise through the Grenadine Islands with a dear friend. For some reason, it felt shocking to me that I would do such an independent thing, but it was also liberating, completely freeing to my soul. I was finally, truly living. We met up with another friend, and we lived like the Three Musketeers; every day was carefree and full of joy out on the open seas.

One afternoon, we had moored in a calm, turquoise harbor, and just about everyone took turns jumping off the bow of the ship. When it was my turn, I got up to the front of the ship and I started to shake. I simply could not muster the strength to jump. In my heart, I wanted more than anything to fling myself off the ship into the clear, warm waters, but something deeper was stopping me. I turned around and watched the others have fun.

Now, I know it was the dutiful me sitting dormant inside my soul telling me this was wrong, this was unsafe, and this was not what sweet girls did. It wasn't a fear of water; it was a fear of my wild self, and a belief in the parental forces that had brought me up and the society that wanted me to live and behave a certain way.

As I began to search inside myself to find the source of this fear, I saw that my upbringing, though idyllic, perfect, and peaceful, had left some deeply embedded beliefs within me that were stopping me from achieving so much. I look back at this time with so much joy, but I also must question those elements that ultimately held me back from achieving a sense of freedom and inner power.

This is not the only way in which we are all guilty of sabotaging ourselves. So many behaviors that we have learned from an early age continue to secretly hold us back from achieving our best life.

Recognizing those beliefs and behaviors is the first step.

## *Chapter 2 Summary*

- "The Dutiful Me" is a seemingly innocent construct that stems from a good place, but it can lead to an adult life that is under-confident and damaging to self-growth.

- Certain things in our upbringing make it so that "rebelling" isn't an option. We become willing participants in a life lived small.

- "The Dutiful Me" stops us from taking those giant life steps that serve to unlock our real potential.

- We are all guilty of sabotaging ourselves, but it is not necessarily our fault. So much stems back to the way we were raised. Unbeknownst to so many people, our parents included, we are training a whole generation of women to live life small.

## *Take Time Now to Reflect*

1. What behaviors or feelings do you still have now that are holding you back?

2. What do you need—internal or external—to start to let go of what no longer serves you?

3. What is one Tiny Moment of Joy you can create to make you smile and laugh, and make your heart sing—if only for a few minutes?

# Chapter 3

## Disney Princesses

As a young girl, I genuinely believed in *happily ever after*. In my own way, I think I still do. Now my version now looks quite different from the wonderland existence I devoured time after time as a child.

Of all the princesses, Cinderella was always my favorite. What I loved so much about her story was not that she created any magic, but that magic simply happened to her. The beginning stages of her life were full of strife, grief, tragedy, toil, and hardship. For me, her princess power was patience. Cinderella waited and waited and waited; she trusted that there was a magical prince out there on the other side of the horizon—and he was coming to her on a horse, riding fast. And if she could just hold on a minute longer, all the pain of her life would be solved. She also had a calmness and lack of negative judgment, even though her mean stepsisters tormented her daily.

She had an abundance of magical friends who would help show her the way to a magical life. Much like me, she followed the rules dutifully, and that decision to conform brought her many gifts: beautiful gowns, a magical pumpkin, a glorious ball, and finally...the perfect husband.

It is all a question of how long can you hold on, how deeply can you trust that your pain will all seem worth it once your Prince Charming arrives. We suffer so that one day we can finally live a dream.

I bought this narrative hook, line, and sinker. I mean, I bought in fully. I was one thousand percent in the cult of Cinderella. Her life was the life I wanted. I was certain good things were not created; they happened to us. Whatever came to us was precisely what we deserved. And most of all, if I was "good," then "good" things would happen to me. And that would be my fate happily ever after.

I did not for one second consider that perhaps one day, this way of thinking would lead to a great deal of pain.

I look back at so many of my decisions, especially the ones that led to darker chapters of my life, and I realize this mentality served as the core motivation for those choices. My first marriage was heavily influenced by the story of Cinderella. It was as if I was playing a part.

Back then, marriage was simply what you did if you were "following the rules." During the fraternity and sorority stages of life that dominated my college experience, a number of rules had to be followed. First, you were "pinned," which quickly progressed to an engagement and then before you knew it, you were married only a few weeks after graduating from college. That was just how it was. You weren't supposed to question if maybe there was something more out there, something that better fit your life and aspirations. That fear of jumping off the boat, of doing something you wanted for no reason other than to exercise your independence—that was not an option for me at that time.

Back then, many of us simply reacted, but something else really important was happening at the same time: Women's Liberation. Bra burnings. I watched and cheered from the sidelines but didn't actively participate. I spoke in support of the movement but took no action. My bonds to being silent were too strong.

I have now come to learn something far different than this way of living.

The truth is, we create our own magic. Magic is not made for us. To wait is to suffer; it is to put aside all of your potential in favor of someone else's potential. It is the opposite of creativity, empowerment, and freedom.

I'm not at all saying that accepting Cinderella stories contributes squarely as blame for some of our sorrow in our modern society; it's safe to say that's quite an overstatement. It's a lovely story and we must all, from time to time, let go and indulge in a bit of whimsy and fantasy. We must also realize that there are real stakes to the narratives we choose to digest, especially at a young age. We must now, in our maturity, look back at these tales with wisdom and experience and ask ourselves what purpose these stories held for us.

I loved my second husband more than I could ever tell you. I love him just as much today. He was my Prince Charming. And I am now only starting to see that he was a companion to my own quest, not a magical fix waiting on the other end of a beautiful horizon to ride forth and save me from my pain.

You are the arbiter of your own destiny. You have a deep power to create the world you want to see. You are magic yourself.

*"If there's one thing I've discovered, it's that stifling yourself will only lead to more misery. I polluted all other happiness because I was afraid to let myself create and change. You have to have courage. Real courage to explore, to fail, and to pick yourself back up again."*
— **Siobhan Vivian**, *Same Difference*

## *Chapter 3 Summary*

- The idealization so many young girls feel toward Disney princesses teaches us that good things happen to us not by us.

- We believe a fiction that if we behave and stay "good," then good things will happen to us in return. This narrative is severely holding us back.

- Growing up in my time, so many life steps were taken simply because "that's the way things were always done." We never asked why. Asking why is something we must embrace today.

- You are the arbiter of your own destiny. You have a deep power to create the world you want to see. You are magic yourself.

## *Take Time Now to Reflect*

1. Do you believe you are capable of creating your own magic? If not, why do you think that is?

2. Do you believe others contribute more to the magic in your life? In what ways?

3. What is your limiting belief that is getting in the way of creating more magic in your life?

4. What is one Tiny Moment of Joy you will create to make more magic in your life?

# Chapter 4

## *The Force of Creativity*

One of the most creative people I have ever known is a dear friend, Starla J. King. She is an author, writer, writing coach, and creativity coach with a lifetime of experience living and working creatively. She came into my life almost seven years ago when we both attended a small-group coaching program focusing on women-owned businesses. Our coach, Lorin Beller, who still continues to be my coach and mentor, not only supported us in our fledgling businesses, but gave us new tools and a mindset for personal growth—for being a "Big Fish" in life and in work.

As we came up together, I had the great pleasure of getting to know Starla's work and mission more intimately, and our relationship greatly changed my life.

Starla's teaching focuses on helping others identify and express their unique "voice" in ways that connect meaningfully with those who need to hear that message. She holds a deep belief in the power of creativity to change our self-experience in a way that gives us and our community greater access to our own talents, inner wisdom, spirituality, and joy. This belief shines through in all the work she does. Having lived for many years believing that creative pursuits were somehow "lesser than," Starla founded her business OutWrite Living, as a headquarters for services that help promote and facilitate the use of creativity as an essential part of healthy, productive, and meaningful living. Starla reinforces the idea that we need dreams and a plan to work toward them. She also helps others to understand that it is essential to create a world without labels and without judgment (toward ourselves or other people), where each person has a right and a desire to access and express the creativity within themselves.

Sometimes we think, I am not creative. *I can't write, dance, paint, act, cook, etc.* What I've learned from Starla is, we must never underestimate the power of creativity.

However, creativity is much more than those skills or activities. *Creativity is all about giving yourself permission to think, feel, and act differently than you ever have before.*

Try this exercise to activate your creativity:

- Think about a time when you gave yourself permission to move into a new direction (pick just one time in your life). When you have that example, and I am sure it is making you smile right now, remember that you do have it within you to be creative. Now is the time to take that and start applying it to doing the things you really want in your life.

- Write this on a big sticky note and put it on your computer, your bathroom mirror, any place that you will see it every day and be reminded that you can give yourself permission to do and be who you need to be—at any time, in this moment now.

### Take Control of Your Own Life

This is *your* life, not someone else's. You get to design and live the life you want and need. Sometimes we hold ourselves back because we have been programmed and don't know how to undo those habits. Sometimes we are simply afraid to change.

Here are some powerful ideas and ways to take control and start designing your life. It starts with reframing your **self-limiting beliefs.** These beliefs can exert a tremendous influence on your thoughts, which then extends to the actions you take.

As for myself, I used to have a lot of self-limiting beliefs:

- Children should be seen and not heard.

- I should marry young because that is what everyone around me is doing.

- I shouldn't ever get a divorce because no one else in my family has gotten one.

- I shouldn't speak up loudly at meetings because I really didn't have much to contribute. (I had this belief until I heard my thoughts said by someone else and then I kicked myself for not opening my mouth!)

These beliefs come from the way in which you view past experiences, from a significant life event or from messages that others may have given you over the years.

"I don't think I can do this. I've never run a business before."

"I'm terrible at public speaking."

"No one will believe in my vision."

"It's too scary to change—what if I fail?"

Now, I bet you're asking the question, how can we move forward from these beliefs? They have their reality *in your mind only,* so in order to shift your thinking, you must learn to reframe these thoughts so that they are empowering. Here's a process to follow that will help you change your perspective:

1. Identify possible sources of the self-limiting belief, to bring it into your awareness.

2. Recognize the experience, event, or messages that may have brought about this belief.

3. Reframe this belief using positive self-talk. Address the "buts" that will inevitably leap up in your mind as you reframe your self-limiting belief.

4. Continue this process until you have replaced your limiting belief with an empowering belief.

Here are some examples of self-limiting beliefs and how to get rid of them:

1. *Self-limiting belief:* "I don't think I can do this. I've never run a business before."

   *How to turn this around:* "Although I have never run a business before, I have done [insert your accomplishments here], which gives me the skills to start. I am as smart, if not smarter, than others who are running a successful business, and I will be successful too."

2. *Self-limiting belief:* "My family always told me that I was much better at creative endeavors than at business. I have no business experience. How will I ever be successful?"

   *How to turn this around:* Use reframing, empowering self-talk, such as, "I love my family and it is also time that I believe in myself and do what makes me happy. My creativity will be an asset as I work to launch my new business. I will connect with those who have business experience to get appropriate advice as I work on my plan."

3. *Self-limiting belief:* "But I've never put together a business plan!"

> *How to turn this around:* Eliminate the "but." Instead, say, "I will work with the local small business incubator to put together a business plan."

This will take some work and real commitment but if you give yourself permission you will let go of all of your self-limiting beliefs. And this makes room for more beautiful things to come into your life.

Author C. JoyBell C. talks about not being "afraid of change." She has a great metaphor that pictures us feeling safe in a small pond. Yet, if we stay there, how the heck will we know about the vast oceans in the world, or the world of space for that matter? Just because it feels okay now, do we just want to settle for okay in the future?

There are so many strong, smart, and powerful women you can learn from. Marie Forleo has inspired me greatly over the past few years. I am in awe of her energy. She tells us to think of fear as just a "type of energy." If we pay attention to it, we can use it as a beacon guiding us where we need to go.

I have learned that when we acknowledge and recognize the feeling of fear, we can begin to move on. We need to focus on what is happening when this feeling overcomes us. We need to stop, notice where it resides in our body and how it manifests within us (for me, my breathing gets tight and I feel a heaviness in my chest), and acknowledge it.

## Commit to Continuing the Process Every Day

Every time self-doubt creeps in to hijack the self-empowering process, be aware that it is happening, acknowledge it, and go back to your positive self-talk. Write down your limiting beliefs on a card, rip them up, throw them out or put a match to them (carefully), and let them go, creating space for something new!

Then write your empowering beliefs on cards or sticky notes and carry them around with you or stick them on a place where you see them every day.

Ultimately, when we accept our creativity and our own self-empowerment, we see that the happily ever after of the Cinderella story is a construct that is only here to hold us back, not bring us peace.

A life well lived is a life of work, of overcoming your personal demons and tragedies and finding a balance in your own existence between the sweetest highs of life and the crippling lows. Beauty lies in that lovely in-between space, not in some make-believe euphoria. Perfection is a construct that seems wondrous at first, but over time will break down and expose itself as a sham. When that rupture occurs, you will be left holding an empty bag.

We must accept now that the only life we have is the one we make with our own two hands. We also get to make it better by reaching out for support to others who can guide us. It is not only okay, but critical, to ask for help. You don't need permission to do so. Building something new requires grit and reinforcements. Get your hands dirty. Work with your team. No need to do this alone! What do you want to see out of your life? Build it now. Not tomorrow—right now.

Will it be easy? Sometimes it will and sometimes it will be really hard.

Will it be worth it? Absolutely yes.

And you can tell the whole world that Marybeth told you that one. If you find within yourself the courage to truly build the life you want, then you can have your fairytale existence. A real one; a fairytale story that you and you alone wrote for no one but yourself.

## *Chapter 4 Summary*

- The teachings of Starla J. King show us that the power of creativity helps us change our self-experience in a way that gives us and our community greater access to our talents, inner wisdom, spirituality, and joy.

- We must never underestimate the immense power of creativity.

- This is your life, not someone else's. Therefore, you get to design the life you want and need.

- Reframing self-limiting beliefs is essential to taking control of your life.

- We must accept that the only life we have is the one we make with our two hands.

## *Take Time Now to Reflect*

1. What are your 2–3 most powerful self-limiting beliefs? Be honest about this. For example: I'm too old; I don't have the right education; I don't have the energy/smarts/freedom to get my dream job/partner, etc.

2. What is the one thing for each of these beliefs that I can do right now to let them go?

3. What support do I need to let them go?

4. In what ways am I creative?

5. How can I give myself permission and allow myself to create the life I want?

# Chapter 5

## Don't Take Your A-Bombs So Seriously

*What are you griping about? It's just an atomic bomb.*

What does that mean? Precisely what it sounds like! Nothing is worth taking too seriously, not even an atomic bomb. This was one of the greatest lessons I learned as a child.

I do not in any manner mean to be callous about the brutally severe world we live in where nuclear weaponry can and has been the cause of widespread destruction, loss, and pain. Nevertheless, there is still great wisdom in this sentiment.

I grew up during the Cold War. That meant that I was away having fun at school all day while the grownups worried and fretted about the end of either Western Civilization or possibly the entire world.

I, however, had more immediate threats to concern myself with: the nuns who ran my school.

Because of the nuns, I knew that every day, my one clear mission was to be a good girl. The result of not being good was a nice, strong smack. Now, I empirically knew that I was a good girl because:

A. I was called on a lot in class.

B. I was never smacked.

I remember a very special class assignment where each child had to construct by hand their own religious altar. *What fun!*

I made mine with my father. He was a wonderful craftsman. We built my altar out of wood, and outfitted it with lovely cloths and a nice little chalice to place on top. We spent hours upon hours in the basement constructing this wonderful piece of art. Despite the immense effort and care put into the altar, I don't remember winning any prizes, although I most certainly believed I deserved the highest of praise for our work. I do remember having fun. I remember spending time with my family. I remember being so proud of this altar. And I owe it all to the nuns.

Despite all the fun of altar building, sometimes the problems of the real world did find a way to interrupt the school day. We had air raid drills—a lot of air raid drills.

Whenever we heard the blare of the siren, we knew to immediately put our little heads under our little desks and hold our faces down, armed with nothing but the steadfast belief that this ritual would somehow keep us safe from the gargantuan power of a nuclear attack.

Sometimes, we got to experience the extended air raid drill. And, as crazy as it may sound...that is where all the fun happened.

My classmates and I would take a journey all the way to the underbelly of our school, through the basement that also connected to the corresponding basement of the nun's convent. This way we got to really hide from the A-Bomb.

While we certainly cared deeply about our safety, what excited us most about this journey was the opportunity it presented to take a peek at the daily lives of the nuns as we sojourned into their personal space. And the most interesting part of this trip, at least to me and my friends, was the laundry lines hanging in the basement that was home to the various undergarments the nuns would wear and, of course, subsequently wash.

I repeat, *the nuns wore underwear.*

What could be funnier to a group of eight-year-olds than seeing the underwear of a nun?

Of course, this was a tightly held secret the nuns did their best to conceal from us. We were instructed not to look at the undergarments as we passed by, and this instruction was enforced by the ever-present and only sometimes effective ruler. And trust me, if one of us was ever brave enough to look at the underwear and let out a giggle, that ruler would come with the fury of lightning.

Honestly, it was so worth it. Times were certainly dark, but those adventures under the convent were some of the greatest and the sweetest I can remember.

As I grew up, I realized that times can always seem dark. I do not know the last time I turned on the news without having the narrative of the end of the world thrust upon me. This is a constant in our life.

I know deep down in my gut, there will never be a moment in our life where we cannot find our own version of the nun's underwear. For my entire childhood, those little white undershirts and big panties were hanging there to bring me joy, even in the darkest of circumstances. In their own way, they are still there today. Some days I close my eyes, and I can see it. And I still laugh like an eight-year-old girl. It's utterly immature and wondrously healing.

Like Dr. Seuss said, "Funny things are everywhere." Be on the lookout. Open your eyes and heart to wanting some fun every day. When I see a dog in a car with its head stuck out a window and the silliest grin on its face, loving every second of life, I just laugh out loud. Laughing actually changes your brain chemistry; it releases endorphins, the body's natural feel-good chemicals. Decide to pick one thing every day to make you laugh and you will instantly feel good.

## *Life Is Only as Hard as We Choose It to Be*

This is not to say that real pain does not occur; it absolutely does. I lived so much of my life thinking that my time on earth was idyllic, perfect, peaceful, and that it would always remain that way. And then one day, the direction of my life completely changed. Sorrow flooded into my day-to-day and I was in no way prepared for it. It hit me so hard that I thought I would never recover.

I can't say with any complete certainty that I have now. Have I recovered? I am not quite sure what that even means.

Recently, I have found myself more at peace. I see the path forward for me, and I have taken many steps on that path. As I put one foot down, the path continues to grow before me. Step after step, I find clarity. I also find joy, inspiration, and best of all—humor.

Humor is infused in every ounce of life. The darkest of days can be wondrously funny. Think of how many comedies brilliantly tackle the subjects of death, sorrow, grief, pain, and loss all the while making us laugh uproariously. That's the beauty of the fine line between comedy and tragedy. The two live with only the tiniest thread between them.

As a child, we were faced everyday with the knowledge that our destruction as a species could come in a flash and that we would not have the time or the means to do anything about it. It was harrowing.

Also...the nuns wore underwear! How amazing is that?

36

## *Chapter 5 Summary*

- Life is only as hard as we choose it be.

- Even in times of the most severe stress, such as an atomic bomb drill, we must find the small bits of joy that help us laugh and get through the dire situation.

- Pain does occur; it is real. Peace, however, can still be cultivated with intentional behavior and work.

- Humor is infused in every ounce of life.

- There is a fine line between comedy and tragedy, and that is where the beauty of life lives.

## *Take Time Now to Reflect*

1. In what ways do you make your life harder than it needs to be?

2. What makes you laugh? What can you practice every day to laugh more?

3. How can you add laughter or find some fun in the "atomic bombs" that drop into your life?

# Chapter 6

## Welcome to the Real World

College was a hoot. There's no other way to put it. I left for college when I was eighteen, and I was the first in my family to go, so we really had no bearing or orientation for what to expect, what to do, or how to navigate what, for us, was a completely new system. The nuns at my high school obviously wanted me to go to a Catholic girl's college, and I was a good girl, so of course I listened and went off to Pittsburg to study at Mount Mercy College, a Catholic Women's liberal college.

Was I nervous? Absolutely!

Was I excited about finally experiencing what life was like outside of Reading, Pennsylvania? Oh, yes.

I was also nervous. The anxiety was terrible.

I remember the first glimpse I got of my roommate Beatrice, a sandy-haired, freckled girl from Boston with an impeccable smile and a really aggressive sense of optimism. She was walking down the hall wearing the most immaculate pair of white gloves. White gloves. Who wore those? Beatrice wore those.

I also remember that she was wearing the most enormous smile I'd ever seen in my life. And I so desperately wanted to be her friend.

Here was this stunning Brahmin girl from the good part of Boston, and then there was me, a skinny Italian/Austrian/Czech girl from a middle-class family. I have learned, however, that smiles go a long way in the department of making friends. So, I tried to smile as big as she did…and it worked.

We had a lovely time together.

I was very joyful then. I chalk this up to those big smiles and an obsession with living every day in the moment. I didn't think about what was coming in the next year; I just stayed where I was. I loved adventures, I loved new people, and I loved finding all the little hidden gems each day seemed to give me.

When it came to my studies, here are the three most important things I learned: abnormal psychology, how to protest, and how to play tricks on your sorority sister. Trust me, these are the things in life that will really take you far.

I know this may come into conflict with the picture I have painted of my life as being centered around nothing but strict by-the-book, rank-and file do-gooderism. I was aware, however, of civil rights and the women's movement, and I did my fair share of protesting and I lived my fair share of life.

It was freshman year. My girlfriends and I watched in pure terror, behind safely bolted windows, as tank after tank, followed by strict lines of soldiers, rolled and marched their way down Pittsburgh's Fifth Avenue.

The day was April 5, 1968. The day before at 6:01 PM, Martin Luther King Jr. had been struck by a single bullet fired while standing on the balcony outside Room 306 of the Lorraine Motel in Memphis, Tennessee.

And now the rioting had begun.

I couldn't understand how the happy dreamworld I was living in could have seemingly been whisked away in a second. All of a sudden, the frivolities of our lives, the identical heather skirts and cardigans we had all purchased with our mothers just months before, the matching dorm linens that were specifically selected to synchronize with our roommates, all felt so useless.

Here we were, right in the middle of riots, burnings, and the bubbling over of deep anger and resentments of a class of American citizenry that had been treated as second class for so many years.

It was a shock, a trauma to my sense of self and my understanding of the world around me.

I did not know how to react. Peeking out of my dorm window at the huge tanks rumbling down Fifth Avenue, I was terrified to my core and I wanted nothing more than the peace and safety of our home, which I would soon get.

Campus was evacuated shortly thereafter, and we were all escorted to the airport. We flew home—numb, afraid, and utterly confused as to what the next step of our lives would be. The snow globe façade of our life had cracked and there was no going back.

After a week or so, we were allowed back on campus. I came back to finish the semester, but I didn't return to Pittsburgh in the fall.

The truth is, it wasn't just that I was so fundamentally shook by the events of April 1968. To be frank, I was quite homesick. I was out of my comfort zone. And maybe, just maybe, there was the incentive of my high school boyfriend to whom I wanted to be closer to. I transferred to a college closer to home, and all the while the world seemed to fall deeper and deeper into chaos.

## In the Time of War

Social war had exploded, spilling into the streets and affecting the lives of countless Americans. The crisis in Vietnam had devolved into pure madness, the death count climbing at immeasurable rates, and all the world seemed to be able to speak of was the unnecessary tragedy American had gotten itself into all the way on the other side of the world.

I remember classes where we never even breached the subject at hand; all we talked about was the war. In physiological psychology, a class normally reserved for discussions on the structures of the brain, rather than discussing prefrontal lobes, we debated the moral merits and failings of the war and the politics behind it. Was it offensive to protest or was it our moral duty? We thought we knew it all, being so young and idealistic.

I was at the forefront of demonstrations against the war.

In truth, I was so young and naive that I didn't know what I was protesting against. I fought against "the war" as a concept, but what thought did I give to those who were actually fighting it, suffering from it, the countless Americans whose lives would forever be damaged by the conflict? I feel a great deal of shame when I look back at this time. The world around me treated soldiers returning home from Vietnam with nothing but pure disdain. They were ignored and discarded like nothing more than an enemy of our idealism.

At the time it felt right. It's what we were being fed night and day. I don't make excuses for this. It's just the simple truth of what happened.

We were the generation of love. We were the flower children. We wanted peace and happiness and for everyone to get along. That was our dream, a vision of the future that would be quickly undone when four unarmed students were shot and killed while protesting at Kent State.

That shattering changed a lot of young people. On one hand, it opened us up to the reality of our situation; on the other hand, it only incentivized us further to live each day with wild abandon. You had to live each day free, because who knew when the hammer was going to fall on us? I earned the name of "Mad Dog"—my wild woman was allowed out for a little bit.

The dutiful me still made her fight. She didn't allow me to fully let loose. For the most part, I still did what I was told in 99.9 percent of situations. My parents were happy and proud of me. Not only was I the first to go to college from our family, but I was making high marks and eventually graduated with honors and a bachelor's degree in psychology.

I quickly married my childhood sweetheart only one month after graduating.

All was going according to plan.

Until my first meeting with a recruiter.

We had just moved to New Jersey, and I was filled with excitement to finally begin my new adventure into full-fledged adulthood. Now it was time to decide what my career would be, a decision that I thought would completely determine who I was.

I had a meeting set up with an employment agency, and I was sure I was going to knock this one out of the park. I walked into the meeting like I had an entire army at my back. I sat up straight, smiled that good girl smile, and then I heard five little words that would quickly and efficiently dismantle and devastate any woman of my generation.

"How fast can you type?"

Hold up. I had a degree in psychology—did he not know this?

I was here to help change the world, or so I thought. In that moment of intense clarity, the world as I knew it exploded. From that moment on, nothing would be the same again. I grew up, and it didn't feel so good.

I laughed straight in his face and told him squarely that I didn't type.

To which he quite succinctly told me, "Welcome to the real world".

So, I listened to him...I joined the real world. And I saw how hard it could be. I allowed myself to be pulled into all that was against my nature. Looking back, I accepted it and did not have the courage to say I wanted something more. I blocked my intuition that all the while was telling me to look for something more. I didn't realize that there was something primal and wild within me that needed to get out. That I deserved a bigger life.

This began many long years of a constant state of settling. Not that I didn't learn—I did, every day! Not that I didn't have fun—I managed to have great fun a lot of the time. The idea of being my authentic self and creating my ideal life was just a flickering thought that came and went in the daily routines of living. There was no creativity in my life.

Many years ago, I discovered Clarissa Pinkola Estés's novel *Women Who Run with the Wolves*. Recently, I started to re-read this powerful, life-changing book with a small group of incredibly smart, loving, and supportive women who are interested in life and learning every day. Dr. Estés reminds us that there is a Wild Woman in each of us. She encourages us, even challenges us to "be wild." Although culture and society put up barriers and block us, we are the ones who have to *"allow it (our wildness) its freedom."* She tells us that only then can we start to be "creative" with our lives.

This book is so life-changing and powerful, and each page is filled with ideas and words that resonate in my very soul. I want to just bathe in it and the lessons and "aha!" moments I get with each paragraph. I am blessed to be reading this with other amazingly insightful, smart, creative, and spiritual energy healers and women who want more! We discuss this book chapter by chapter and learn that each of us has an innate knowing that if we continue to push down our creativity, we get to a point where we cannot keep ignoring what it is we are meant to be. Our story must be told—not only to ourselves, but to the rest of our world.

We are the only ones stopping ourselves. We block our joy—no one else does. When we admit this, it becomes our very first step to finding joy every day. I could spend the rest of this book talking about the Wild Woman, and I will come back to it in later chapters. Consider getting this book and immersing yourself in it with others so that you can start to let out your Wild Woman, your authentic self.

## Chapter 6 Summary

- Life can often hit us by surprise; one moment, we are living in an idyllic dreamland, only to be immediately thrust into the pain of reality.

- Growing up is painful. Living through history is painful. Life itself can be extremely painful, but there is always a way to choose joy.

- The moment you hear, "Welcome to the real world," can be a painful incident in anyone's life. Please understand that you get to choose what "your real world" is.

- Embrace your WILD WOMAN. Let her stories be told.

## Take Time Now to Reflect

1. What do you love best about the real world you are in?

2. What do you like least about your real world?

3. Take time now to acknowledge the Wild Woman, the authentic you. How would you describe that person?

4. What is holding you back?

# Chapter 7

## Why Not?

Fast forward a few years and I found myself smack dab in the middle of the 70s. It was a fun time, a time to explore and to play.

The adventures of my first marriage took my then husband and I from New Jersey to Chicago, and it was the first time I really experienced the differences, the advantages, and the struggles of metropolitan living.

When the pitch to pack up and move clear across the country came our way, all I can remember thinking is, "Why not?" As I look back now, I see that "why not" is a question that has really come to define a great deal of the decisions in my life. For the most part, good things came from asking, "Why not?"

To this day, I love the question. I love the freedom to say, "Yes," rather than buckle down underneath the weight of a thousand seemingly good reasons not to do something wild and adventurous. I love the escape "why not" brings us, I love the opportunities it brings, and in its own strange way, I even love the headaches that sometimes come from it.

In this instance, moving to a cool, hip, exciting city like Chicago, taking a new job with a promising new career path, meeting new friends, and living in my first high rise—all of these elements were too attractive for me to pass up. While I can't say they didn't live up to the hype, I did quickly learn that "cool Chicago" was really a "cold Chicago." That terrible weather didn't stop me from taking my new urban existence by the horns and grabbing every last ounce of fulfillment and adventure I could from it.

It was the strangest experience to exit a bustling Chicago street into the quiet chamber of my apartment complex. I would silently take the elevator all the way to my apartment. It was as if this magical place was shielded away from the bustle I knew was raging beneath me. Walking into my apartment felt like walking into a cocoon.

The first thing I always did was run to my large living room window. Below was a stunning view of the Lincoln Park Zoo. I loved watching the small people and cars zooming to and fro like ants marching. The sight made me feel safe. It also made me feel like a grown-up. I was free; I could do whatever I wanted—I could finally eat ice cream for dinner.

I had taken a job in Human Resources for a chemical company, an organization that, up to this point, was mostly populated and run by men. I was the only woman in the department, and though I expected a fair bit of bullying, what I received instead was an unbelievable amount of care and attention. Someone was frequently asking if I was okay, if I was comfortable, if I needed anything.

I'm loath to admit that honestly, I enjoyed the attention. The men were a fair bit older than me and the relationships were fatherly and innocent. It was all fine in my book. They were looking out for me and frankly, I believe I needed that.

It's a bit crazy, thinking back, how different the ecosystem of the working world was then. The "9 to 5" of the 1970s today seems like a vestige of a bygone era, with so many practices that now seem so foreign. Taking work home was utterly forbidden, and long lunches? They were a requirement.

Our offices were located directly across from Sears Tower and only a hop away from Greektown. On a regular basis, the entire department would take a sojourn over to our favorite Greek restaurant. Even more regularly, we would decide to just call the day "quit" there. The boss was normally with us, so that decision came straight from the top.

We ate amazing flaming cheese, we suffered lousy Retsina, and we drank glass after glass after glass of Ouzo.

I don't mean to imply that we didn't work hard; we absolutely did. It's just that back then, we knew how to balance it all out.

The work (and the play) soon began to pay off. After some time, I was designated to designated to work directly with the VP of Engineering, assisting him in hiring a new batch of chemical engineers.

This designation was not something the VP was happy with. He had little faith in what a woman could bring to the table. To be honest, this field of study was something I knew absolutely nothing about. I had garnered a reputation as a quick study, and my new boss mentored me with an outstanding amount of patience and really brought me along. I talked with engineer after engineer, and it wasn't long before I really started to understand this stuff. Dare I say, I became really good at it.

Ten months later, my boss asked me to come see him in his office. I began to have flashes of my meeting with the New Jersey recruiter. Did I do something wrong? Was I not meeting expectations? Did I need to go back to typing?

Thank God the relief came pretty quick. My boss told me that not only was I doing a fine job, but that Emil—the VP of Engineering— had firmly stated that he did not want to work with anyone else. That was quite a big swing from his early proclamation that no woman should be a part of the Engineering Department. What lesson did I take away from this? Focus on being your best and don't let others' definitions of you limit who you are.

Before I knew it, Chicago had squarely become my home, and it would happily remain that way for several years. I don't know how else to put it—life was just...fun. There was little stress, and I made enough money not just to live but to live well. To play. To truly experience this amazing city. My only regret from this time was that the intoxication of the city wrapped me in so tightly that I did, to some degree, ignore other vital parts of my life. I would call my parents probably once a month, when the loneliness of being away from my home community really set in. Those were rare moments.

I imagine this hurt them. My parents were always so supportive, and they never would have dared to intrude on the success and enjoyment I was having in my new life, no matter how much this hurt.

Never once did they bring this matter up. To this day, it's one of the greatest regrets of my youth. Community and family had always served as a cornerstone for my upbringing. Yet, I was so quick to abandon it for some shiny, new future that was halfway across the country to completely upend my life.

I was never able to address it openly, but knew that every day I had with them was my chance to show all the love I had. I learned from them that when there is unconditional love, past hurts are forgiven. It was such a life lesson that I hope I have been able to pass on to others as well.

### *Chapter 7 Summary*

- Life can move fast. Frequently, we accidentally leave our loved ones behind in the flurry.

- Work can always be done to repair relationships. Nothing is final. Everything is in our control.

- A youthful life in the city moves fast; opportunities come and go and you meet so many amazing people along the way. Staying true to yourself is what above all matters most.

## *Take Time Now to Reflect*

1. What were the times in your life when you said "Why Not," and reflecting back, they turned out to be some of the best decisions you ever made?

2. How did letting loose and going after what you wanted make you feel? It's very important to describe this—don't just say "fine" or "good." Dig in and remember what it really felt like—if it made you feel energized, made you smile, feel like you were fully alive, etc.

3. What did you learn from this letting go?

4. What stops you from letting go now?

5. What are one or two things you can do to go for "Why Not"?

6. Are there relationships you need to repair and find forgiveness? Sometimes it is not possible, but how can you forgive yourself and move forward?

# Chapter 8

# The Polar Bear Cometh

Chicago was amazing, but man, the winters could be tough. In this town, winter lasted from October to May. It was long, painful, and for my East Coast blood, it was a real big shock to the system.

It was especially difficult as I was working right by Sears Tower, and its massive height would create gigantic downdrafts that would make Chicago feel even more brutal. The city would fasten metal poles and ropes all along the sidewalk so we had something to grab on to. Without those, citizens could truly get bowled over by the force of the gusts.

Every morning, we woke up and listened to the Frost Bite Report, a daily ritual that would tell you not only the temperature, but also approximately how many minutes it would take for your skin to freeze.

At first, this crazy weather had a sense of novelty to me. It was fresh and fun in its own strange sense. Over time, it really started to get to me. I mean, my favorite plant was a palm tree. So, living in the tundra took a toll on my spirit, my health, and my happiness.

Because we lived in Lincoln Park, right on Lake Michigan, we were directly across from the famous Chicago Zoo. I loved that zoo, especially the orangutans. I loved them so much that I would visit them a few times a week when I got off the bus right after work.

What I loved most was the way they cared for each other. They knew a few simple truths, some that I think we all need to take a refresher course on. These orangutans knew how to serve one another, even in the simplest ways. Sometimes, all a fellow chimp needed was help removing some bugs from their back. Sometimes, all they needed was a big hug.

I loved these animals. I always felt it put us humans in perspective. They taught me so much, to have a simple life and check on each other, for bugs of a different kind.

No animal taught me more than the polar bear.

One particularly cold day, I was putting on my whole winter weather get up—the extra sweater, the long shearling coat, the heavy-duty boots, all the scarves, my hat, and my gloves. It was an exhausting process just to get dressed.

As I put on my winter armor, I caught a glimpse of a breaking news alert. It said, "For anyone living in Lincoln Park, stay indoors. Do not walk, get your bus, or go near the zoo."

Don't go near the zoo? Oh no!

Apparently, during the night a pipe had broken and formed an ice bridge large enough for a polar bear to climb out and take a little stroll.

I'm going to say the obvious here—if you have ever seen a polar bear, they are humongous and terrifying. Their feet, their teeth, and particularly their heads—all of it is totally frightening. Think paws about a foot wide with sharp claws ready to rip you apart.

I watched from the safety of my apartment as the city did their best to capture the polar bear. All I can say is, the polar bear gave them a run for their money. In the end, they safely obtained him and brought him back. The whole affair filled me with a great deal of wonder and sadness. A large part of me was rooting for that bear.

Honestly, I admired so much about that big furry snowball. Zoos have always enthralled me, but they also filled me with a sense of longing. I would observe as these animals would find every ounce of joy they could from their life. Ultimately, underneath their exterior was a sense that they did not belong here. Their home was somewhere far different than this and their life had taken a course that was in reality a gross deviation from where they were meant to be.

When the polar bear saw that ice bridge, I like to believe she realized this was an opportunity to return to the place she was meant to be. She didn't wait. She took immediate action. She climbed out, she took the city head on, and followed her own north star.

There is an old saying, "You gotta play to win." If you choose happiness, success, curiosity, love, or whatever it is you desire, you can't stand on the sidelines. Being frozen in place, waiting and waiting until something happens to you, will not bring you joy. It does the opposite.

The delay is what takes so much of us away from our purpose. A biting sense that there is a better time to act, a better time to take that huge step forward in our lives, a better time to do the thing that is clawing inside us. It is that feeling that blinds us from seeing the ice bridges forming all over our world. They are everywhere. We just have to open our eyes to see them.

Animals take little for granted. They are honed in so fundamentally on their goals, wants, and wishes, and like a heat-seeking missile, they find and immediately act upon any and all opportunities to seize their desires.

It was time to go home.

To this day, I envy that ability.

The world has clouded us from our own instinct and judgment. I do believe that we have the same abilities as many of these animals, many of the same instincts and the same deep resonance with our life purpose. The current construct of our society have made those instincts foggy. It is as if we are seeing it all behind a veneer, a cloudy shield that tells us it's okay to wait on our dreams, that there will be a better time to do it in the future. Only when we have more money, more support, more experience can we truly do the things we were put on this planet to do. We let these lies hold us back.

The polar bear failed at her great escape. It's an image that still haunts me to this day. I sometimes fantasize about going back to that zoo, breaking all the animals out, and letting them run free back to their home in the wild. I want that freedom for them so deeply that it eats away at my soul.

I knew then, watching those city workers take that poor animal back to the zoo, that I would never fall to the same fate.

## *Chapter 8 Summary*

- The story of the polar bear teaches us that we must all create our own opportunities and seize the moments life puts before us.

- Animals take little for granted. They are so honed in on the present, their goals, their wants, and their wishes that they are ready to immediately act on the opportunities they are given.

- The world has clouded us from our own instincts and judgment, but we can re-cultivate those abilities.

## *Take Time Now to Reflect*

1. When is it time for you to let go? To accept and move on.

2. What are you holding on to in your life that is dragging you down? What delays you from making decisions that will bring you joy?

3. What values do you hold most dear in your life that you have hidden and need to honor now for you to move forward?

# Chapter 9

# If You Want to Dance, You Gotta Pay the Band

My first husband and I quickly found jobs and moved back to New Jersey so we could be closer to our family. However, it wasn't long before we came across an unnerving realization: our marriage had cracks in it.

I'm sure you may have noticed that I strangely haven't said much about my first husband to this point. There is a reason. We simply were not compatible. We did not have a deep relationship. The truth is, I don't have much more to say.

We suffered from a phenomenon that many women of my generation fell into; we got married too young. At that time, marriage was a box that needed to be filled by a certain point. To ensure you hit this timeline, often you had to settle. It was just the way of the world.

When I said, "I do," my husband and I were both far too young to understand the stakes and consequences of those two words. I remember getting ready and putting my veil on, and I had this feeling deep in my stomach that said, "This is a mistake. Don't do it!" I remember quickly putting that feeling away—too late now! I was getting married in an hour, so there was no turning back. Talk about the consequences of not listening to my inner self!

My husband and I were both too oblivious to understand the importance of those choices. We were in love...or so we thought. If there's one thing I have learned, it's that youth really does have a knack for blinding us from the veracity of the hard facts of life, and there's absolutely nothing we can do about that.

Pay attention to what your instincts and your inner voice are telling you!

In *Women Who Run with the Wolves*, Clarissa Pinkola Estés tells us to "practice listening to [our] intuition." I think the word "practice" is really important; she doesn't mean just once in a while. It is a discipline, just like learning tennis or playing the kazoo (now that will make you laugh), that raises our awareness and makes us better! Taking that practice inside, we at first have to consciously be aware of our feeling, our intuition, that little voice nagging us. I have learned, as I am sure you have as well, that when I ignore it and push it down, I get into trouble. Dr. Estés says these "powers were given to your soul at birth." Stay alert to what your heart is telling you.

When we came back to New Jersey, we realized something fundamental: we were entirely different people. I had gone down one path during our time in Chicago; he had gone down another. We were splitting further and further from each other with each passing day, and the marriage was beginning to lose any sense of meaning or hold.

Then he decided to end it.

Looking back, I can see that it was absolutely the correct choice for both of us. In the moment, it was impossible to view the situation with any wisdom, maturity, or patience. All I felt was anger...so much anger.

He had met somebody else and wanted out. In my mind, all I saw was a cheater and a quitter. My blood was boiling, my anger was growing to insurmountable levels, and that's when the wild woman came out.

I wanted payback.

I decided that he could get out if he wanted, but it was going to cost something. My mantra became, "If you want to dance, you gotta pay the band." I was the band and it was time to pay.

I wanted everything and I got it. The house, the belongings, the personal valuables...all of it...and all that vitriol came with a nice little addition: I got the mortgage as well.

## *Chapter 9 Summary*

- Ignoring our instincts can only cause pain. They will not go away and we must face them head-on so we can move forward and grab the joy that is waiting for us.

- Revenge doesn't help. Being honest with ourselves is our best choice for growth.

- The "good girl" in me trained me not to ask questions and to never ask why. This led to a first marriage that lacked depth and companionship.

## *Take Time Now to Reflect*

1. What were the times in your life when you ignored your instincts?

2. What were the consequences of that?

3. How can you be better at listening to your inner voice that will guide you to better decisions? What do you need?

# Chapter 10

# Welcome to the Real World Part 2

With the divorce came a lovely little notification from the bank that since the house was now mine, I was also the sole owner of the mortgage. That was no problem at all. In fact, I was ecstatic. I wanted my name and my name alone to belong to that house. This couldn't have been better.

Then I went and met with the bank. Once again, I got slapped in the face by this tricky little thing called reality.

The banker told me quite abruptly that since I was now the sole proprietor of the mortgage, they would be exercising a small print clause called "the right of acceleration." In essence, this boiled down to two things: either I had to pay down the mortgage immediately, or I had to sell the house.

The news couldn't have fallen on me any heavier. It was like someone had ripped the ground out from underneath me in just a few seconds.

The anger came back again. The wild woman ripped right out, just moments away from tearing this banker to shreds. I asked a simple question: "Do you also apply this rule to all of your male customers after their divorces, or do they get to keep the house?"

I thought his mouth was going to drop clean to the floor. He sputtered like a broken engine, asking me what I meant. So, I clearly and plainly stated that I was questioning whether the bank had discriminatory policies toward women. If this was the case, wouldn't that be an interesting story for the paper?

He sputtered off again and said he would have to get back to me.

The next day I received a letter with the paperwork attached to sign the mortgage over to me, no strings attached.

I had won. The wild woman inside me did it. She came out in full force and surprised us both. I don't know where she came from, but I know that she had always been living there, deep inside the recesses of my being.

That's where we come back to playing small. So many women have been taught to remain tiny, to keep everything bottled inside. I now see it's because the world is deeply afraid of the power we hold as women. Once we release the wild woman, everything is at our disposal.

She lives inside each and every one of us.

We all have the power to change the world. We all have within us a deep well of power. We are not victims to our circumstances; we have the energy to push back against them, to enact change and to create the world we want to live in.

### *What Is Your Desire?*

To be your best self, the woman you really want and need to be, you must start understanding how powerful your *will* is.

One of the readings that has been a beacon to me for the last decade is a verse from the Upanishads, a collective of Hinduism texts written sometime between 800 and 500 BC.

*"You are what your deepest desire is.*

*As is your desire, so is your intention.*

*As is your intention, so is your will.*

*As is your will, so is your deed.*

*As is your deed, so is your destiny."*

For me, what this boils down to is—we need a plan, a template to understand where we are and what factors might make it difficult for us to find that deep well of strength and vision to move us forward. We must pay close attention to the messages we send to ourselves and the actions we unknowingly take that keep us from making any progress.

As you journey further along toward your destiny, it's essential to define the resources that will help you to move forward, as well as any obstacles you will need to overcome. Taking the time to define resources and obstacles will help you create a more realistic picture of the actions you will need to take to make your Destiny Vision™ a reality.

Both resources and obstacles exist on two different levels—internal and external.

*Internal Resources* – qualities, skills, or experience you possess that will help to further your Destiny Vision. For example, the accounting skills and patience you developed in your last job might very well help you create a financial plan for your new endeavor.

Destiny Vision is a powerful Program at The Center for Women's Leadership that will help you define what your limiting beliefs are and create a practical and exciting action plan for you to be who you want to be. See our website for more information.

*External Resources* – elements of your plan that you will need to access from other sources. As an example, perhaps you'll engage a professional to create your website. It helps to take a creative approach to these arrangements; they need not always be costly. Students can often be hired for a variety of services as they are trying to break into their fields.

*Internal Obstacles* – the limiting beliefs that you carry around with you. That voice telling you that you won't get there, that you're not competent. These obstacles are often more challenging to overcome than external ones. You will need to work on reframing the powerful self-limiting messages you send to yourself so that they are expressed as even more compelling self-empowering beliefs.

*External Obstacles* – the barriers outside of yourself that you must overcome in order to reach your Destiny Vision. Perhaps you're having a tough time finding grant funds to start that organization, or the workspace you thought would be available fell through. If you are willing to share the external obstacles you are facing with others in your network, quite often putting that feeler into the world will bring about new ideas, approaches, and possibilities.

The first step to joy is awareness. Once you have identified your obstacles, you have taken that first big step to move forward.

## Chapter 10 Summary

- Women are taught to play small. The world is deeply afraid of the power we hold. Once we release the wild woman inside us, everything is at our disposal.

- We all have the power to change the world; there is a deep well inside us all. We are not victims to our circumstances. We have the energy to push back, to enact change, and to build the world we want to live in.

- To be your best self, the woman you really want to live as, you must start understanding how powerful your will is.

- To do this, you need a plan—a template to understand where you are currently and what factors might make it difficult to find the deep well of power and vision inside you.

- Defining the resources you have available to you, both internal and external, and the challenges that are facing you will be instrumental to enacting this plan.

### *Take Time Now to Reflect*

1. What were the times in your life when your Wild Woman took over and you stood up for what you believed and needed?

2. How did that feel? (Again, be very descriptive.)

3. How can you cultivate that power within you? What do you need?

4. Be aware of your own obstacles. What are they in each of the categories above?

# Chapter 11

## He-Peating

After the divorce, my life didn't stop. It began. I dug down deep and got creative, because the pain was too much to stay the same. I had no choice but to live my life again, by myself. It was a time of exploration—a time to meet new people, take trips to NYC with girlfriends, stay out all night, and live life. I remember one time in particular a group of about five of us girls decided to head to the city to check out a new Brazilian dance club. All I remember was we had way more than one cachaça, the national drink of Brazil, and how we got home safely, no one knew. I guess our guardian angels were working overtime that night.

I let loose. I actually allowed myself to be carefree and happy and to enjoy each day. That investment in my independence and love paid me back tenfold. I began a new job, and eventually, I met the love of my life.

If I hadn't allowed myself some space, some new adventures, some joy, I would never have found love or what would become a very successful career. During this time, I met so many wonderful people. People who greatly influenced me and brought me love and happiness.

In my new career, I had a far larger role than before, managing a staff of HR employees, many of whom are still my friends. There were certainly challenges, but I saw the world was giving me more space and more opportunity to continue growing.

I began to work for a company that made the most decadent, delicious ice cream in the world. How much fun was that! But the corporate culture? That was more challenging than I imagined. We were owned by a large British conglomerate and therefore, they brought young, anointed men into the company to run it. Being a young woman, I felt quite intimidated. I felt I had no power at all.

Alice Walker, author of *The Color Purple*, writes about how people are the ones who give away their own power "by thinking they don't have any."

As I began my new career, those tapes of "children should be seen and not heard" began to play again, over and over in my head—no matter how empowered.

I felt this fundamental lesson was still sticking around, spreading like a virus and touching so many facets of my life. It is what I thought. What I learned from Alice Walker is that by thinking this, it becomes our reality. My reality that I am responsible for. No one else.

I remember boardroom meetings where I would find myself stuck in the middle of what seemed like a never-ending sea of men in suits. I would make commentaries, ask and answer questions, and give what to me felt like valuable input. To the rest of the world around me, however, it was nothing more than the whispers of ghosts. My words seemingly disappeared into thin air the moment they came out of my mouth. This is how I felt for the large part of my time working with this company. I accept my part of the responsibility for my behaviors.

Then, all of a sudden, I began to notice that my words were being heard. They had to be...because the next guy sitting right beside me would parrot the exact sentiment, verbatim. And of course, the moment he said it, the whole room would erupt, nearly vaulting to their feet with applause. "What an amazing idea!" They may have well been giving the guy an Academy Award. I guess it's not the idea that matters anymore, but the mouthpiece...specifically, the gender of the mouthpiece.

I hear that this is a common phenomenon amongst women, and that today it's been given a name: "he-peating." God, do I love that.

There is no question that for a large portion of my life, I was "victim" to the scourge of "he-peating." At the time, I had no idea what to do about it. I would just sit there, encircled by all these corporate men, completely numb, without a shred of agency toward my own thoughts and actions, nothing more than a victim to this toxic culture that was holding me back. With each board meeting, I found myself shrinking more and more. I grew quiet, reserved, a shell of myself. I now know that it was how I came across as well—I talked quietly, without conviction.

Silence soon became my method for self-defense, a necessary tool for ensuring my self-preservation and the elimination of pain.

I began to think that this wasn't a problem with the world around me, but instead a problem with me as a woman, as a person. To a degree, I guess I did deserve some blame. Where was that wild woman I had just so recently found? Why had she all of a sudden grown dormant? Why couldn't I release her once more to tell those jerks, "Hey, listen to me."

As I was beat down further and further by the actions of those around me, I let their behavior turn me into a different person. My speech and my actions began to reflect my internalizations. I grew quiet and spoke without authority, and this only set off a cycle of a perpetuating behavior where I communicated to all those around me that I was nothing more than a doormat, ready for them to walk over me whenever it pleased them.

I knew I was smart; I knew I had strong, wise things to say, but I wasn't presenting myself as if that were the case. I wish to this day

I had some kind of support—a coach, a mentor, just someone who could smack me upside the head and say, "Get a grip, girl, and let that wild woman out!" This lack of accountability and support was a lesson I would learn much later on, but at that precise moment, I couldn't have needed it more.

The he-peating continued on and on and on and on. Though the effect was to cripple my sense of identity, to cast me into a deep cycle of self-doubt and depression, it also set off a spark of determination. Somewhere deep within all that pain was the tiniest little light, glimmering in the darkness, telling me that if I just held on, I could do better. Perhaps, one day, I could, in fact, change all of this.

I knew full well what I was capable of; I just didn't know how to accomplish that vision.

As I developed on my journey to actualizing all of that potential, I couldn't help but look back at the early times in my life and shake my head. If only I knew then what I knew now. If only I had the control then to let my true power out, to speak up, to take action, to create the change I wanted to see. We all have a deep reservoir of abilities waiting inside us, if only we would give it the permission to release.

I didn't know then what I know now. I was where I was, and my journey needed to continue.

## *Chapter 11 Summary*

- Silence becomes a method of defense against the phenomenon of "he-peating."

- Giving in to this phenomenon strips women of their power and sets off a cycle of self-perpetuating behavior.

- This can cripple our sense of identity and create a cycle of self-doubt and depression.

■ Somewhere deep inside all of us, there is always a source of light reminding us of our strength and power.

## *Take Time Now to Reflect:*

1. What were (or what are now) the times in your life when you feel you were/are not heard?

2. How does it make you feel when you're overlooked?

3. What do you think is the root cause of this? Be brutally honest— is it how you come across? Are you being overrun in a man's world?

4. What are one or two things you can do to overcome this?

# Chapter 12

## A North Star

While my life to this point certainly had challenges and disappointments—a divorce, difficult moments that I needed to overcome—the course of my life and my understanding of myself took a drastic change with the death of my mother in 2008.

At the time, I was working for a large international client and needed to take some meetings in New York. I was walking down Park Avenue, feeling pretty pleased with myself, feeling a bit like I was (almost) actually making it in this world. I was on top of everything; I couldn't be stopped. Everything was going according to plan, and the road in front of me was nothing but bright. Then my father called and told me I had to get to Reading right away. In that moment, I knew exactly what he meant.

How could I go from such a high to such a low within a nano-second? Maybe I wasn't meant to be that full of myself, or that happy. Maybe, just maybe, I was finally paying for that happy childhood, the bad side of the karma, the re-balancing of everything.

My mother had bravely battled Parkinson's for twenty-two years. However, in the last five years of her life, the disease took a drastic turn, and it finally won.

My mother handled it with a grace that can be described in no other term than saintly. She never once complained. She saw her disease as a part of life, as a part of God's plan. Of course, she wished the circumstances weren't so, but she still took every moment of her journey with a quiet acceptance.

My father embraced the role of caregiver with a strength that to this day still absolutely astounds me. For all those years, he stayed diligently by her side, giving constant and loving care to her. He took no regard for himself; all his energy went to her. It was in those moments that I truly understood the depth of love he had for her, the strength of their relationship. Even in their most challenging moments, their love only strengthened. They did not bow under the pressure. They grew.

I sat beside him as often as I could, watching him as he fed her, as he cared for her every need. Each meal could take as long as an hour, but not once did I ever see the smallest glimmer of impatience. I was in such awe of him, never once realizing that I would need those skills.

Eventually, Dad passed away from mesothelioma contracted during his time in the Navy. Simply put, there was so much pain. I still feel his loss and wonder why such a good man had to suffer so much. I have come to accept these sad times in my life. This was how their lives had to unfold, and how the family got to learn from what unfolded.

In all this time, never once could I see that there were so many lessons swirling around me. I was too wrapped up in the grief and the pain and the loss. It would not be until years later that I could look back at these instances with any sense of clarity and wisdom. When my second husband, Harry, wrestled with and later succumbed to his own illness, he showed his courage in facing and accepting what was happening to him. Harry and my dad are both beacons of light, my "north stars," because they were truly selfless. They did whatever they could to accept the reality and protect our family from their fears. They sought out their tiny moments of joy— laughing at "Hogans Heros" or "Beverly Hillbillies." Being so happy when I made my homemade spaghetti and meatballs, or the crabcakes I was famous for. Their love and appreciation spilled out to the rest of us and we were lifted up even in our sorrows.

If only I could have seen these moments for what they were at the time. They were there for me to grow and prepare for the litany of challenges that were waiting right on the other side of this corner of my life. The pain in the moment can, without considerable practice, blind us from the truth and the lessons of our circumstances.

Amit Ray, author and spiritual master, tells us that we need to leave things behind if we "want to fly in the sky." To grow, we have to "let go [of] the past that drags [us] down." Letting go is really hard sometimes, until we make the decision to do so. When we do, it opens up space so great things can fill in where there was hurt or pain before.

We can indeed practice. We can grow. We can learn to see all of our challenges as moments of growth and opportunity for taking that pivotal step toward becoming the person we've always dreamed of being.

It just takes work to allow your better self, though not work in the sense of drudgery or some difficult uphill battle. To be better takes curiosity and allowing yourself to experience life with wide-eyed openness. Commit to this work and allow your best self to flower into a journey of joy! One of the most powerful things you can do is think of this journey as a cleansing, to open up new spaces within so you can move on and be better each day. This is a commitment to loving yourself.

## *Chapter 12 Summary*

- We all have a north star in our lives, even in the most dire of circumstances. This north star will always point us toward our strength.

- Pain can blind us from the truth and the lessons we are meant to learn during our time on this earth.

- We can practice finding truth; we can grow. We can always see our challenges as moments for opportunity to continue taking the pivotal steps required to become our true selves.

### *Take Time Now to Reflect*

1. How do you normally deal with your emotional or spiritual pain? Write this down.

2. What is effective?

3. What is not effective?

4. What can you do to react to this pain in a different way— one that you see as a growth opportunity?

# Chapter 13

## Falling in Love

had not prepared myself for the difficult times that were to come in the continuation of my story, save for the passing of my mother and father, an inevitability that will be experienced by the majority of humans on this Earth. Having grown up with so much security, so much love, that idyllic sense of wonder, in its own way, blinded me.

It also drove me to something.

After the failings of my first marriage, I knew now that I wanted the same sense of peace, partnership, and support that my parents had enjoyed for so much of their lives. I knew I wanted it, and I knew I would find it.

I am so happy to tell you that I was correct. I did find it. I did have it for a time, and it was idyllic. No strings attached. No buts. No changes to the story. I fell in love, and I was gifted with a partnership that can be described as nothing short of a blessing.

I met Harry through work. This time, I was working for Thomas' English Muffin, a hundred-year-old company that was on the advent of a huge boom, growing from a successful mid-Atlantic company to a national brand. He was working in the corporate headquarters and I was in a division. From time to time, we would have meetings together, and little did I know that all the while, he was falling for me. He was falling for me big time.

At first, I thought it could be possible that he was a corporate plant working as a spy, because I believed at the time that his boss did not think much of my boss (I had a bit of an overactive imagination back then).

After a few meetings, he finally asked me out on a date. I was reluctant. At the time, his boss at headquarters didn't really like us at the division because they were very buttoned-up corporate and, well... we were a bit crazy.

Our division housed very alternative types of teams and management theories. We tried all kinds of new ways to grow and become a better company and workplace. This didn't always sit well with the buttoned-up corporate types—hence, why I believed Harry could have been sent as a spy, to gather dirt on my boss. This did not sit well with me. I was fiercely loyal to my team and my boss. I liked what we were doing. I didn't want it to change.

However, from the moment he picked me up, that reluctance was all but wiped away. That man knocked me off my feet. He took me to one of the hippest restaurants in New York City, followed by a night at an even hipper disco.

Truth be told, I was sort of dating somebody else at the time. Okay, I was absolutely dating someone else at the time. In fact, that man had just professed his undying love to me. So, I guess I could say I was in a bit of a sticky situation.

What was I to do? I was falling in love. That's something I have learned you shouldn't take lightly.

Harry was the man I had always envisioned myself with, and here he was.

Everyone who was lucky enough to meet him during his life described him as kind, happy, and loving, an innocent troublemaker who knew how to have a good time and how to raise up those around him. Everyone who was lucky enough to truly know him and to call him a friend knew that these impressions were true. Time only made them more secure. He was consistently kind, patient, and fundamentally good.

I got my Prince Charming. I got my Prince Charming for thirty years. Perhaps I should view that as a gift.

There are so many women who don't get this life for a second.

Unfortunately, thirty years was far too short for me. I think a lifetime with him would have felt too short as well.

## Chapter 13 Summary

- Falling in love can always happen, even in the most unlikely of places and situations.

- We must express gratitude for the love we have in the time we have it. Love is a gift when it arrives in our life, no matter in what form.

## Take Time Now to Reflect

1. How can you open yourself up for more joy? Write down everything you can think of so that opportunities for happiness come your way and you are ready to receive them.

# Chapter 14

# Passing the Baton-Your Legacy

Dara Horn, an American novelist and professor of literature, writes about how, "Every person has a legacy," and how even though we may not know it and we may not become famous for it, we do have aftereffects. I think often about how we never know what our impact will be on others in the world.

Harry and I got married, and a few years later we were gifted with the incredible surprise that our family would be growing to three. Completely unplanned, but completely what we knew would fulfill us even more. All I remember about that day was an overwhelming sense of unbridled joy. When I am at my lowest points, I put my mind's eye back on that day. The emotional resonances immediately come back to me with so much vivid life. I am able to put myself back into my body and mind at that moment, and it brings me such joy.

Together, we had a beautiful daughter who, to this day, astounds me, surprises me, and pushes me to be the best woman I can be. I didn't realize that my mother's love for me would almost instantly transfer to my little girl.

All my hopes, dreams, and work felt at once like they belonged to her. It was a beautiful moment. I began to realize the power and responsibility we hold as mothers, and the immense duty we have to prepare the generations coming after us.

Dr. Tererai Trent, the all-time favorite guest of The Oprah Winfrey Show, once told a powerful story detailing the power and the responsibility of passing our knowledge and love through generations. Dr. Trent was born in Zimbabwe, growing up in unfathomable conditions. Her life was a journey that would see her beginnings as a goat herder evolve into a Ph.D, an ambassadorship with the U.N., and a mission building schools all across her country, expanding the educational reach of her country and fundamentally shifting the lives of countless children just like her.

At age fourteen, she was married off and, by the time she was eighteen, she had already given birth to four children of her own. All the while, she had one dream driving her: to receive her education, to take the best of what her mother and her grandmother had taught her, and to move forward. She did not want to simply "take the baton," as she called it, the baton being the lives of the generations before her who had accepted the poverty, stagnation, and lack of movement that had come to define so many women of her country.

Dr. Trent had created a legacy for those who came after her. She decided that the future for her children and for women all over the world had to be different than hers.

We leave a legacy behind in everything we do. We also have a duty to give those who come after us an opportunity to change, to take their future into their own hands, and to ensure that the lives they live are not mired by the lives we lived.

Our legacy, **our sacred responsibility**, is to be that role model—to teach, to encourage, to show our daughters and sons, colleagues, friends, and family how to live the best life they are capable of. The ways to do this are simpler than you could ever think.

1. **Be kind always** – At the end of your life, do you want to look back and know that you were always "right" about everything, or that you were kind—always?

2. **Fill your heart with love** – For yourself first and then others.

3. **Dance everyday** – Even if you are sitting down, put on your best dancing feet—under your desk, in the kitchen, in the grocery store, dance every day. You can't be stressed or sad and dance at the same time. Marie Forlio said, "And if we would all dance there would be no war." How true!

4. **Bless and release** – You are not going to like everyone. People will press your buttons, if you allow them to. They say and do stupid, mean, and terrible things. Most of the time we cannot change that. We can only send them blessings and release our reactions, release our judgments that what they do is good or bad.

5. **Stop judging!** – It serves no purpose to judge others. Why do we feel we have the right to condemn or criticize when what we need to do is try to understand, or show them different options?

6. **Look for options** – They are right in front of us.

7. **Have gratitude for each minute, each experience, each person** – I've found out that the people who annoy us the most are those we learn the most from.

8. **Choose joy** – EVERY DAY.

9. **Choose today** – You can't live in the past and the present. Know that as much as we would like to turn back the clock and do things differently, it doesn't work that way. Do you know how many times I have relived the choices I made—if only I had nagged my husband more to go to the doctor, if only I had done x, y, and z, then he would still be alive today. During those moments of wanting to change the past, of the regrets, I miss out on how I can be happy right now.

10. **Get out of your comfort zone** – We are not here to be cozy and complacent and settle for "good enough." We cannot live each day by being just good enough. That is not why we are here. We are here to be our BEST.

## *Chapter 14 Summary*

- There is a great power and responsibility we hold as mothers.

- The story of Dr. Trent teaches us the importance of legacy, and that the future for those who come after us is created in our present.

- We have a duty to those who come after us to create the opportunity for change.

- Our legacy is to be a role model and to teach and encourage our daughters, sons, colleagues, and friends how to live the best life they are capable of.

## *Take Time Now to Reflect*

1. What do you want your legacy to be? This is one of the most important questions you can ask yourself. Put aside some real quiet time to answer this.

2. How do you describe yourself now? Is there a gap?

3. How do you want others to describe you? What do you want them to say about you now and at the end of your life?

# Chapter 15

# Is This It?

Elizabeth Gilbert, one of my most beloved authors and human beings, is an astonishing, courageous, smart, and inspiring woman. She talks about grieving, and how one day we will realize that although we mourned, we were in change; "Your heart was broken, but your life was changing...."

Thanksgiving used to be one of my most favorite holidays. There was always a warmth to it—family, laughter, smiles, and comforting, homemade food from recipes handed down from grandparents to parents to us. There was no pressure for gifts. It was truly a day of gratitude.

One Thanksgiving, all of those good memories and feelings were suddenly replaced with fear. That day was the beginning of a heart-wrenching chapter in our lives that would end six years later. My husband had a massive heart attack, which would require seven bypasses and a long and difficult illness that would eventually take him away from us in 2017.

It has been a few years and yet I still have a very difficult time discussing this fully and publicly. It is so personal and private and I don't know if it is helpful to anyone to relive those years. To be truthful, I have been stuck in my own writing on how to get through this part of my life in a way that is helpful or inspiring to others. So rather than go through the many days of fear and hardship—physically and emotionally—I will highlight moments that I hope inspire you.

There were many days and nights during my husband's illness and following his death that forced me to ask myself—Is this *it*? Is this what life is supposed to be? Is this what his life, and our family's life, is supposed to be? There was nothing in my life that prepared me in any way for this level of sorrow, loneliness, hardship, and finality.

Up until this point, I had been so blessed with such a joyous life. I remember one friend saying to me how blessed I was to have been so adored and loved by my Harry—and yes, I am grateful beyond measure for that. Having such an incredible gift taken away from me also makes the loss that much harder. Does that make sense?

We were supposed to retire to someplace warm with palm trees...to travel like we always loved to, planning our next vacation during the one we were on. We always had something to look forward to. We were the best adventurers together, not climbing mountains or living in the rainforest, but being in magical Italy, flying through the canals of Venice on a vaporetto, the wind in our hair (he did't have much, but it still was flying backwards). Laughing, looking at the carved bridges and gargoyles, being in awe as we gazed up at the dizzying ceiling of Cathedral San Marco. Or relaxing in the soft sand of Hawaii, with the blue waters and pink skies at sunset, and always with a tropical umbrella drink in hand. It didn't matter where we were. We lived each moment together. We were our own life's joy—just being together. Seeing our beautiful daughter laugh and learn to ride her two-wheeler down the sidewalk. Watching her grow up so happy in our little seaside town—she and I were the girls with our long hair flowing as we rode our beach cruisers all over town (the whole one square mile of it).

It was a fairytale. My happily ever after story that came true.

For almost thirty-five years, each day was one of love—not always easy, but always joyful. I knew I had met the true love of my life, and we were so blessed with our beautiful daughter. Our little family.

When Harry had his heart attack, lost his kidney function, went on dialysis, and then was placed on a transplant list, not only a heart, but a kidney as well, we were still hopeful. We had been told he had four to six months left, then maybe a year...and then one year turned into two, then three, then almost four...and we still had hope...until one day, we didn't.

After all that waiting, being good and compliant, and never complaining, one day he died suddenly. Then, there was no more hope. The hole inside of me was a physical hole—a total feeling of something empty that would never be filled again. It was totally and completely over...the beautiful life we had together. No more looking forward to our retirement together; no more flying and holding hands together on the airplane smiling and waiting to see how our trip would turn out. No more dinners with our dinner clubs. No more family dinners or trips to Reading or feeling the joy of getting gifts for each other for Christmas or birthdays or Valentine's Day. He loved to buy us gifts and flowers...even for no reason. Now, no more, no more, no more....

By this time, our daughter was grown and living on her own, working in Manhattan. She stayed with me for the first several months, and talked to me every day thereafter, but in my day-to-day life, I soon had to get used to being on my own. I was faced with questions like: Do I put out two towels or just one? How do I not set two places at the kitchen table? When I go to the food market, do I order two pieces of chicken or fish because then I don't feel so lonely getting just one? When I ordered takeout, it was now a small order and they always said, "Is that all?" When I came home from a business trip, I wanted to get out my phone and say, "Honey, I just landed, I'll be home in an hour." Now, I was greeted by an empty house instead of being hugged and kissed and held tightly. I was lonely from the inside out. I thought—Is this it?

In writing this book, I would like to tell you that at this point, my life has gone back to a fantastic dreamland— that I have moved on, met someone, and am now living a life full of happiness and ease, but not all of that is true. Yet. Yes, I do move forward, and even though there are challenges every day, I have more strength and determination every day to reflect, to be aware, to ask myself, "How can I feel better and make better choices today?" This is how I choose how I am going to spend each day—in joy or in pain? In openness or remaining closed to life? Do I have to work at it? A bit, but the more we practice, the more we integrate and the easier it gets. Choose to create a habit of joy. It is in your hands.

The pain lessens more and more over time. The hole in my heart is healing and I am aware how important it is to look for the joy, the gift of each moment. Now that it has been more than four years, I have developed some practices to remind me and move out of my pain.

### *Tiny moments of joy to see me through each day:*

- **Stop and breathe.** How are you breathing— shallow and quickly or taking long deep breaths to calm down?

- **Be AWARE of how you are feeling**. What kind of look do you have on your face? What are your voice tones—hard, sarcastic, or loving and kind?

- **Meditate.** Develop this practice for twenty-one days and you are on your way.

- **Take joy in nature.** Look out the window and see the sky, the birds, the flowers, and the trees. Your heart can't help but to sing.

- Be grateful for everything in your life, no matter how small. Set a timer to do this every few hours. This again becomes a practice of love.

## *Chapter 15 Summary*

- Tiny moments of joy are the only way to combat grief.

- Stopping and taking a breath, meditating, looking out the window and taking in nature— these are the ways we bring gratitude and peace into our life, no matter the circumstance.

- Life, even at its apparent worst, is still full of joyful moments. It is up to us to seek those moments and hold on to them.

## *Take Time Now to Reflect*

1. Who are the angels in your life?

2. Do you reach out to them and thank them in whatever way is best?

3. Write down what you want your anchors to be (or what they already are) to help you in the hard times.

4. What are two things that will help you to empower yourself and choose joy?

# Chapter 16

*My Angels*

Throughout it all, throughout all the pain, and even when Harry passed away, there were angels everywhere.

During his Celebration of Life, hundreds of people came together. He wanted a party. So, that's what we gave him. It was funny because as people came into the party room, many believed they were in the wrong place. There was so much joy and music and laughter and singing, they couldn't believe this was the site of what to most would seem a somber affair.

Yet that was how he lived life, and we learned from him.

We played the song "Humble and Kind," which described Harry perfectly. He always had a laugh, a joke, a hug, a kiss, a kind word. I remember one day he was at the mall by himself and he came home in tears. I asked him what had happened, and he told me he saw a mother smacking her little boy. He went to her, told her to stop, and hugged them both because he could not stand to see anyone being hurt. This event affected him so deeply that he continued to cry, even in the days following the event.

How he lived his life was exactly like that—with love—and kindness, we would learn, was the essence of his love. That essence is what I miss. Every day. Each of us who knew him have been touched forever by his goodness.

As that joy of life lingers, I realize how truly blessed I have been in my life, to have him for the time we spent together. I realize, too, that even in the darkest days and nights, human angels were everywhere. I remember a woman who cleaned the halls at the hospital who would come up to me every day and give me a hug and say a prayer. She was an angel. They were everywhere.

The everyday kindness that flowed into me made me realize how incredibly lucky and blessed I was. My heart swells with my deepest gratitude for the support, prayers (especially the prayers), and the sustaining food on those days when taking care of myself was an impossible task. I'm grateful for the people who left me Tastykakes, soup, scones, emails, cards, letters, notes, and flowers. I'm grateful for my friends and family sitting vigil with me and giving me cold martinis.

These angels got me through the darkest of days, and their support continued along my journey.

I didn't expect the second year after his death to be harder than the first...but it was...so much harder. After the third year, I started to find peace, and even now, the daily joys are more and more.

The angels are still here.

Despite the outpouring of love and support, I soon had to face the truth that my life had been turned upside down. This was a trauma, and life would never go back to the way it was before.

Now, this realization of my new life has become final...my new reality. I accept it and tell myself how really and truly exceptional a life I have had so far. Many people go through their whole lives never knowing love—not the real kind—and I have had days and months and years of love aplenty.

As my husband battled the wrenching illness that he would eventually succumb to, I made the decision to place my focus entirely on his fight. I made the decision to be with him and to give him my all. I made the decision to pour every ounce of my energy, time, and heart into his healing. I certainly missed out on "things"—events, work—but they were the unimportant things. That was clear to me.

Putting my husband first wasn't just something I wanted to do; it was something I needed to do. It was a calling. There was no other alternative. This man was truly the love of my life. The bond we forged together over thirty years of marriage was so unbreakably strong that I knew this was my moment to step up for him. While we inevitably lost him in February of 2017, I do not regret an ounce of my decision to be with him until the end, to fight with every last bit of strength in my body. It was so much more important than being at a meeting or writing a report. I can look back and be content that I made those choices.

He was so full of life and so full of love, and he shared that love with everyone who came into his life.

I try to be aware now of how I spend my days, of how I treat people, and I always strive to choose to smile instead of being angry. It is the highest tribute I can give to his memory—to continue to show his great love for others.

I know now that I am so truly blessed to have been gifted with year after year of unconditional love. That is something many people do not get to experience. What we had was a rarity, a gift, and something that has so profoundly affected my life for good, even though our time together was cut short.

Of course there is a void left behind. The void is so deep that I am only now starting to fill it back up, one moment at a time. It was a slow crawl, and a long journey, but one that is flowing more freely now. Sometimes, I am still angry, and I am still grieving, and my heart stops when I hear our favorite song or go to a restaurant we loved. The sight of couples walking together hand in hand still makes my tears begin to flow. I am lonely. There is no getting around that.

However, that is not the end of my story—not even close. For inside this journey, there have been so many lessons, lessons I am still learning to this day. I'm reminded of the phrase, "The best is yet to come."

I have learned from this experience that I am made of the tough stuff, the grit that we all have inside of us in unlimited reserves, waiting for us for those times when we need it the most.

This journey has taught me to exercise gratitude, to slow down, to always work to place things into perspective and to never sweat the small stuff, to trust that God is giving me what I need and that there is a plan and a meaning behind my pain.

Now, I look to my daughter as my rock. I reach out to her for support. The angels are there; we just have to look. We just have to exercise our gratitude for their presence and their love. Most importantly, we must make choices to empower ourselves every day, to live our best life in each moment.

### What Is on Your "To Be" List?

This sorrow and loss have taught me so many lessons and brought me further along in my journey than I ever thought possible.

I remember one day I was organizing my desk, and an old envelope fell out of some papers I had put aside. On it, I found a quote—written hastily, most likely at an airport waiting for a plane to places unknown. It was a beautiful summer day filled with sun and beach, and I was trying to decide how I would approach the day when I came across this quote. I knew I needed to focus on my work, but my restless self wanted to run out to the ocean...or look for the incredible butterflies on the flowers outside and the clouds floating in the bright blue sky.

Then I found my answer in these words written on that paper scrap:

> Tom Peters—most known for his book *In Search of Excellence*— tells us: *"Celebrate what you want to do more of."*

So, I decided to spend the day celebrating the simple fact that I was able to write that morning, that I was able to get the word out about my business of helping women transition back into the workplace, and that I was happy about all the wonderful women whom I had connected with over the past year. Maybe I would even be content to stay in my office! I found that focusing on the important things helped to center me and keep me focused on what I wanted to do.

I want to do more of these things. It makes me feel good, like I have accomplished something, and it brings joy to others as well. I want more of that!

If you find yourself restless, distracted, and longing to do something (or anything other than what you are doing), and you really want to celebrate more of what you want, I have found that this helps:

1. **Make a very focused list** of what you must get done right now and today. Set time limits, get a task done, and check it off. It is a really good feeling to cross a task off the list.

2. **Create a "To Be" list.** How do you want to feel right now? For the rest of the day? Then choose and decide how you want to live your life today. *Celebrate how you want to be today.* This is even more important than your To Do list.

3. **Celebrate what you are doing.** *Choose those things and people that make you happy.* Do a great job on that report you need to finish. Write that blog. Help someone out who is struggling. Turn on some music that makes you feel good, dance a little

(or a lot), eat some food that tastes so delicious (sweet summer cherries or cold ice cream), stick your toes in the water. Give someone a hug. Be grateful. Do whatever it is you want more of.

The *Bhagavad Gita*, an ancient Indian Yogic text, says, "It is better to live in your own destiny imperfectly than to live an imitation of somebody else's life with perfection." Give yourself permission to be imperfect and take control of you and your life!

Create who you want to be. Don't let anyone else define you. You get to choose! Stop the need to be perfect—perfect doesn't exist in the real world. Take that off your plate and you will feel lighter. A friend of mine mentioned how hard it is since her kids are at home and she has to help them with their homework, and that she feels like a failure because she is not really good at that. She said she feels she needs to be perfect for them, but she just keeps getting frustrated. I looked at her and said, "will remember is not that you couldn't help them with their math problems but rather that you were there with them with love. They will only remember the love."

### *Chapter 16 Summary*

- Throughout life, there are angels all around us.

- As the joy of life lingers, we must realize that we are blessed every day. In every moment, there are blessings.

- Angels will get you through the darkest of days, but it is up to you to identify and find them.

- No matter how hard life appears, no matter how things seem to only grow worse and worse, your angels will always be there.

- Celebrate what you want to do more of. This is how you create the life you want to live.

- Create a "To Be" list, a notation of all the things you envision your life to be full of. This is a crucial step to manifesting and creating the world you want.

- Give yourself permission to take control of your life. You are the only one who can do this.

### *Take Time Now to Reflect*

1. Write a "To Be" list for yourself. How do you want to think, feel, and be each day?

2. What are the top priorities in your life now?

3. Given the state of our world, what do you do differently?

4. Do you have a need to be perfect? If so, identify when those times are and how to respond differently.

# Chapter 17

## It's Not Done Yet

I get a little nervous that time is flying by, knowing I am not as young as I used to be.

Most of us remember that great scene in the movie *My Cousin Vinny*, where Marisa Tomei plays Mona Lisa Vito and says, *"Well, I hate to bring it up because I know you've got enough pressure on you already. But we agreed to get married as soon as you won your first case. Meanwhile, TEN YEARS LATER, my niece, the daughter of my sister is getting married. My biological clock is [tap, tap, taps her foot] TICKING LIKE THIS and the way this case is going, I ain't never getting married."*

For some of us women over fifty, there seems to be another biological clock ticking, and that is the internal need to do something meaningful with our lives. As the years start to fly by, all of a sudden, we are fifty, fifty-five, sixty, and it hits us in the face—how much time do I really have left to do what I really want? We hate to bring it up to ourselves and to others because it is scary, or we have somehow gotten comfortable and it seems like it will be too much effort and energy to pursue another path. Our own foot is going tap, tap, tap. We feel something in our gut that is not right, not comfortable, and we may be able to ignore it for a while, but it will never go away.

That feeling, that voice, is trying to tell you something important. If you don't listen to it now, then when? It is our spiritual biological clock—the one that has always been inside of us, telling us we are here for a purpose. It is our job and our need to find our purpose and destiny. That clock will keep ticking; your foot will keep tapping. So, it's up to you, when you are ready, to listen and respond. You may even find yourself tap-dancing and smiling away as you start on your path to being happy.

You need to ask yourself, "What am I waiting for?" List your reasons, obstacles, even excuses. This is a powerful exercise to confront what is stopping you from acknowledging the Voice inside you. The Voice that says you are here for a reason—to be joyful and bring joy to others—to find the best way you can do that. Don't let fear or self-doubt hold you back from bringing forth this beautiful, incredible person inside of you who is just waiting for your permission to let her out.

I now know that success in life comes from what and whom I love. My deepest gratitude is to the love of my life, Harry, who helped me enjoy life every day. I have been blessed more than many people have, with the unconditional love and joy that we had together.

My gratitude is for my mom and dad. I miss them so terribly even now, many years after their deaths. I know that they would be so proud, not just my accomplishments, but of me as a person. Considering both of them grew up during the Great Depression of the 1930s, and since they only completed high school, they were so happy for me to be the first in our family to graduate from college. I am grateful that they were able to see me at the beginnings of a successful career, starting my own HR consulting firm and beginning a professional journey that would take me all over the globe. My great sorrow is that they died too young. I know they wanted to spend a lot more years with us, and I will miss them forever. I wish I had finished my cookbook, which I dedicated to them, while they were still living—because they were the ones who showed me not just how to cook wonderful, homemade food, but also taught me the importance and blessings of having family and friends at the table. They would have been especially proud of knowing I am an author as well. When I read the stories and letters from women whom I have helped, I always know that George and Dot are looking down at me and smiling.

What do I want to accomplish in my life before the end? I want to keep being a "student of life" (as my life coach would say). I want to learn every day, to stay on purpose and live happily. I still want to wear my red high heels, go to China again, live in Italy or Hawaii for a while, be surrounded by my family and friends, and just be open to new adventures regardless of my age. I want to smile more every day, dance more every day, and get joy from the little things in life so I can give back to others. I don't know how I could want anything more than that.

> *"I want to write and own my own story, and I have started to do just that! I know now that the wound is the place where the light enters you."*
> **—Rumi**

Brené Brown gives us great counsel when she tells us that owning our story may not be easy, but it is "not nearly as difficult as spending our lives running from it." We all have courage within us, and only when we use that courage "to explore the darkness will we discover the infinite power of our light."

Age is merely an external number, and it's not the important thing. What is important is how we feel inside and embrace whatever is going on right now. Feel alive and curious about what is next. Look in the mirror, first thing in the morning without your makeup or hair done, and say, "You are one good-lookin' woman." (It'll make you start the day with a laugh!) Facing life straight on is another tiny joy you can be in control of each day.

## *Chapter 17 Summary*

- For many of us over the age of fifty, another biological clock begins to tick. We begin to feel a great desire to do something meaningful with our lives. This is our spiritual biological clock, and it is a very powerful one. Listen to it!

- What are you waiting for? There is no time like the present. Create the life you want now.

- Continue existing as a student of life. This is a beautiful world, with so much available for us to explore and enjoy. Dive in fully.

- Age is merely an external number. What is more important is how we feel inside and what is happening to us in the present.

## *Take Time Now to Reflect*

1. What worries do you have, if any, about getting older (no matter what your age is)?

2. What do you want to do that you have not already done? Be specific here.

3. What are your ideas on how to make that happen?

# Chapter 18

## Learning to Just "Be"

You've probably heard the famous quote by Anita Roddick (founder of The Body Shop) about the impact a small mosquito has on you when you are trying to go to sleep. Even the smallest things we do, or say, have impact. Conscious choice in our words and actions will make our interactions memorable to others.

How memorable is up to us.

You know how it is—sometimes you just connect with another human being. You feel their energy; it inspires you, makes you smile and be joyful, and gives you such a positive jolt. The opposite is also true; a rude or indifferent remark can sting you. These impacts can happen in a millisecond.

Which leads me to a question—**what message, what energy are you putting out there for others?**

Do you realize that you affect others in unknown and unconscious ways? Just a tiny interaction—a smile or a frown, a word of encouragement or scorn—has untold effects on others. Many times, you never even realize what impact you have as you deposit your energy (positive or negative) on others. Your smallest behavior can be like that unseen mosquito, which leaves a mark long after it leaves.

We are all so caught up in our own feelings and issues. I sense that we are moving toward such an inner focus that *we miss so much around us*. Our culture emphasizes "me" and has a continuous stream of contests and competitions as to who is best and who is worthless. It becomes a lot about how does this affect me; how can I win at this; how can I outshine everyone else, without taking into account how our actions and words affect those around us, people who could truly be helped by even the simplest thing we say or do.

I am sure you have heard the quote, "At the end of the day, I would rather be kind than right." At our deepest level, it is kindness, honesty, and helping others that really make a difference in all of our lives. So, if you want to impact others in a positive way, it starts with awareness. Get out of the space inside your head, stop playing your old records all the time, and feel what energy you have and are giving off.

We complain about how no one listens to us, how people ignore us or blow us off. Do you do the same? We long for meaningful relationships with others, be it at the grocery store, our workplace, walking down the street, or in our personal lives. To have truly authentic interactions, instead of asking, "What's in it for me?" ask different questions of yourself:

- What does the other person need?

- How am I treating them—my vocal tones, my eye contact, my attention?

- What message am I really conveying to them?

- How will they (and I) feel after our interaction is over?

My friend Starla J. King has a wonderful book called *Wide Awake Every Day*, which I highly recommend and treasure. In one of her stories, she talks about being "in uniform." She asks, "What do your emotions, facial expressions, thoughts, and actions suggest about your inner state and your consideration of those around you?" Those words—**"in consideration of those around you"**—really caught my attention. Starting today, be "in consideration of others."

One of my favorite quotes in the world comes from Maya Angelou. She writes that no matter what you say or do, the only thing that "people will never forget (is) how you made them **feel.**"

You can mechanically move on to something or someone else, or pause to be aware of how you impact others. I encourage you to be your best self. A tiny effort of awareness on your part will leave a lasting and wonderful effect on someone.

So, go out today, and each day, and make them (and you) feel good.

## *The Journey to Joy*

When I began this book, I had an expectation that I would reach its conclusion and experience a breakthrough, an opportunity to share with you how I overcame my perceived insufficiencies and my challenges. I thought after penning the final word, I would be overcome with a spirit of happiness and set forth on a life filled with nothing but joy, jumping out of bed each day with a fully defined sense of purpose and drive and contentment. I thought I would be able to tell you I'd met a wonderful man to fill the void in my heart and that we were now traveling the world together as I one day dreamed.

I would love to tell you all of that, but I cannot.

The reality is, I am still very much on this journey toward healing.

I still worry; I am still lonely; I am still hurt at the sight of couples around me. While the pain has dulled slightly, I know it is still sleeping inside me. It wakes me up at times, but now I have acknowledged and embraced the gifts all of this has given me.

Every day there are improvements, small steps on the way to healing. Today, I do smile more, dance more, work more, and sing more. I have found a way to listen to myself and to those voices from deep inside my gut; they tell me very important things. I have found an avenue to speak up when the small biting pains rise up. I have found a way to voice my pain and reset myself when I feel as if I have gone astray.

*My Realizations:*

- Each day is going to happen, with or without my awareness of its possibilities.

- I must face my challenges, do my Wonder Woman stance, and say, "Bring it on."

- My strength lies in my ability to admit that I am still on this journey, that I am not complete, and that I will forever work toward what I want from my life.

- I cannot do this alone. I need a coach, a mentor, and a trusted team of family and friends to guide me along my new path and see how it opens each and every day. I have a tribe behind me—visible and invisible.

- What am I waiting for? I have right now, this moment, to take control and design my life. No one else can define me. Only I get to do that.

When everything seems impossible, when the path before me seems murkier than ever, I have learned to follow a set of four actions that inevitably bring me a sense of calm: set goals, follow up, course correct, and most importantly, laugh.

It is all up to me, and I have learned not to be a victim, nor a persecutor, and that I don't need saving. Buddha said, "No one saves us but ourselves. No one can and no one will. We ourselves must walk the path."

One of my favorite books, one that saw me through my darkest of times, is *Napkin Notes: On the Art of Living*. In it, author Dr. Michael Durst offers a beautiful gift to his readers by discussing how joy can stem from taking "100% responsibility for our actions," showing us how no one can actually make us feel anything. It is within us to decide how we react, what we say, and what we feel. Being aware and intentional is where we hold the power to create our own joy and freedom.

It all comes down to choices. Each new day gives us a fresh start to do something different on our path to being our best self.

### *How to Switch off Auto-Pilot*

I am reminded that so much of our day is spent in a kind of trance. You know—we drive from one place to the next and have no idea how we got there. We put something away and a few hours later we don't remember where it is. It gets a little scary sometimes—is my mind starting to go? Is this what it is like to get older? I read once that being forgetful as we age is really due to the fact that we have so much more stuff stored in our brains that it just takes longer for us to find it. I really like that explanation.

Beyond just forgetting things, I am really talking about how we drift through our day without conscious thought. Like we're on auto-pilot. How often do you...

- interact with someone in a store without making eye contact?

- have a phone call while checking your email?

- check your text messages when having lunch with someone?

- make decisions without thinking through the consequences?

Sometimes we barely register what the other person is saying on a phone call. Our vocal intonation really reflects our lack of engagement. We unconsciously treat wait-staff like they barely exist. We give them an order, don't look up, and then when we need something, we can't remember what they look like!

We make fast decisions because we are just too overwhelmed to spend the time to think through them. A wise mentor of mine once told me to always think through the outcome of the outcome. If I make this decision, whom and what else will be affected? It is a really powerful question to ask yourself. It always produces better answers and decisions. This is an immediate way to get out of auto-pilot.

When we drift through our lives, not only do we miss out on truly being connected, but others miss out as well.

How does your indifferent voice or lack of human connection affect the other human being you are involved with, even if that connection is only for a few minutes? Are you telling them they don't have much value to you, or that you are more important than they are? Is that your intent? If not, stay awake.

Our voice and body language have tremendous effect, and it takes the same amount of energy to really engage as it does to be indifferent. Watch and listen for how people react to you. Your message gets reflected back. Be aware of the feedback so that you can be alive every single day.

Live this week in full awareness, not in a trance. You can **give the gift of yourself** every time you come in contact with others. Be fully aware of your output, your behavior, and your energy. Make sure what you are giving others is the best that you can do and the best that you can be. This is also the ultimate gift to yourself.

### *What Can You Do on Days When You Can't Find the Joy?*

Have you ever had someone ask you a question that made you stop in your tracks and think, *"Wow! I never thought of that!"*?

A dear friend posed one of those questions to me: ***"What do you do on the days when you can't find the joy?"*** All of us have had those times when we have just had it, when we want to run away, when we say, "Why me, God, and no more!"

Many of us face more than our fair share of hard times, loss, unexpected challenges, and disappointments. It can become totally overwhelming, shutting us down and even paralyzing us from being productive or happy. You know—the kind of events that make some of us just want to stay under the covers and hide. At other times, these situations become self-destructive or fill us with anger and terror—not a pretty state to be in. When we go there, it is so hard to dig back out again.

I really had to think about her question long and hard. All of the really basic, and sometimes trite, responses came out: "One day at a time. Live in the moment. This too shall pass." While all true and important, they somehow feel too removed, or over-said, to do any good when you really need a springboard to that joy you so desperately need.

So, what do you do?

> *"Go find your joy. Whatever that is, go find your joy. Are you going to have a good day or are you going to have a great day? Because it's completely up to you."*
> **—Sandra Bullock**

Here are my best, simple ideas you can use every day to help you remain uplifted, in action, and to see the sunshine again. They are little "experiences" that become truly "meaningful" and will bring you more joy each day.

111

1. **Take action**, even if it is to move your body. Lift your head and look up, get off the chair, go for a walk, take a class, listen to music that moves you. Sit outside and write your little heart out. Start that journal. Meditate. Sing or dance. Do or see something new.

2. **Set a time limit.** I find this is a really effective way to get yourself out of your funk and find some joy. Set your alarm for thirty minutes, or ten minutes, or better yet, for five minutes. Let go of the drama. When the buzzer goes off, get up and physically move yourself. Physical moment creates different chemicals and feelings in your body. Be aware of your feelings and how you are moving, from not so good to okay to maybe even great. It is pretty amazing once you focus in on it and feel the changes taking place inside of you.

3. **Find support.** You cannot do this alone. By yourself, you get stuck in the space between your ears—just you and your negative thoughts and feelings that tend to feed upon each other. Reach out for a support team—a trusted friend, a life coach, a counselor, someone from the clergy—whomever you feel comfortable with. Find someone you trust who can help you to laugh a little and move on.

4. **Do** one or ten things that make you smile.

5. **Do** one or ten things that make someone else smile.

6. **Reach out** and find someone who needs help and then help *them*.

7. **Treat** yourself to a little joy—a piece of chocolate, looking at photos that make you smile, calling a friend, watching a favorite movie, listening to wind chimes or a sea shell, or smelling flowers. Use all of your senses.

8. Repeat steps 1–5 as needed. Be committed and dedicated to being in joy every day.

By taking these simple actions, you start to get rid of your feelings and behaviors that no longer serve you, and instead build a new habit that nourishes you and others.

We all have, and will have, incredible challenges and not-so-fun times to face in our lives. There is always beauty in a storm. It is up to us to lift up our eyes and find it. It is not so hard when you know what to do. **Joy is closer than you think—it really is right there inside of you.**

## *Chapter 18 Summary*

- Learn to "just be"—it is a key to happiness.

- Finding joy is a forever action. We are never "complete;" we are never finished. Happiness comes when we accept that each and every day we must awaken to the truth that only by actively seeking joy will we ever obtain it.

## *Take Time Now to Reflect*

1. How do you come across to others when you are not your best self? How do others see you?

2. What can you do to be more aware of the reactions of others— of how to be mindful that this is not just about you?

3. What are three "little joys" you can do for yourself every day?

4. What do you need to do to make a commitment to these changes?

# Chapter 19

_Laughing with Yorself_

"Laughter is an instant vacation."
—Actor and comedian, Milton Berle

I've been parallel parking all of my driving life, but one morning I was meeting a coaching client and had to find a spot on a busy street. There were two places and both looked plenty big enough to fit in. I tried the first one; I lined up and then hit the curb. So, I tried it again. After four attempts, I gave up and moved up the block to the other larger spot. Piece of cake! I lined up again, swung in, hit the curb again and again, and again. Did the curb get bigger? Was there something in the road? I was normally good at this, but not today. I noticed that there was an older man on a bicycle waiting for me to pull in, sitting on his bike looking somewhat amused. I just looked at him and started laughing at myself. Then he started laughing—with a big, wide, toothy grin and smiling eyes—the kind of moment when you just stop and share how funny life can be.

I must have put on some show, because my husband happened to be driving down the street in the opposite direction, was stopped at a red light, and saw what was happening. He later told me that traffic was backed up behind me, people were laughing, and he started laughing, too. You never know how your little moments and challenges can make someone else happy, even if just for a minute.

What could have been an exercise in frustration or embarrassment instead turned into such a happy and perfect moment.

So, I asked myself, why did I so easily slip into joy instead of impatience or frustration? Lately, I had been making more of a conscious effort to do these three things:

1. Take in things as they come—be accepting, not angry or impatient.

2. Be aware of what is going on and find the goodness in it.

3. Stop being so hard on myself (and others).

I think this was a moment when conscious awareness turned into unconscious response. I know that if we practice being more joyful, and less uptight and intense, good feelings just start to happen naturally. Our bond with each other is in our words and behaviors. They are totally contagious, so let's make them be the very best we have. Laugh each day—it's a very good way to "pass it forward."

### *Your Best Self Is Also Found Outside of You*

When we look outside of ourselves, we find the most amazing stories of others who have thrown away self-doubts and limitations and reached deep inside themselves to let their joy and gifts come out.

I recently found the story of Janet Echelman, an artist and sculptor, who changed the ordinary into the extraordinary, but considered herself an "unlikely person" to create what she did. However, she went ahead anyway. In that, she created such amazing, moving art that delights and amazes people on almost every continent because she did not let the "unlikely" part get in the way of what she was gifted to do.

Because of this, she was able to share her best self with the world.

How many of us consider ourselves to be unlikely, unavailable, untrained, untalented? We need to delete the "un" part of these words we tell ourselves and others. Many times, they are excuses for being scared or unwilling to do something new. We tell ourselves it is okay to stay in our comfort zone. Many times, it is not okay. Over time, it becomes not only boring but terribly sad to see all of our potential unused.

In some of my previous writings, I've discussed the *potential and capacity within us*. I am so amazed at how much raw ability, talent, willingness, and energy we have inside of us, especially as women. We must acknowledge our capacity and use the desires and talents we have within. Promise yourself and make a plan that you will commit to re-discovering (or discovering for the first time) all that you have within you.

In her first TED talk, Janet Echelman said, "I didn't know where to begin, but I said yes!" Give yourself permission to say, "Yes!" to doing something you really want to do— to that little voice within that encourages you to learn more, take a risk, and make a decision to be happier.

This is the perfect time to say, "Yes!" and take action in creating the amazing history of your own life.

### *You Can Choose to Both Lighten Up and Light Up Your Life*

I recently read an article on social media that had some tips about traveling light. It talked about leaving those extra ten hair products, and those seven pairs of shoes you will never wear, at home. After all, you are on vacation—travel light!

It got me thinking about all of the extra baggage many people carry around every day. We stuff our emotional luggage with that hurtful thing one of our girlfriends did to us five years ago. Or that failed relationship or marriage and how unfair it was and how terrible that person was to you. We fill up the bags with resentment for someone who got a promotion that we thought should've been ours. The workplace becomes something to dread. Add some envy for that beautiful new house your best friend just bought.

We can't live fully in the present or even move forward with the tons of "stuff" we choose to carry around. If we keep piling it up inside of us, at some point, it will become toxic and we will start to become bitter, jealous, and really unhappy.

*We do have another choice.*

Instead, we can use these life lessons, no matter how small, to learn how to move on and create a better self and a better life.

I always wonder what the point is of rehashing all of the bad stuff in life. The truth is, no one really wants to hear your sad story all of the time—in fact, I don't think even you want to hear your own tale of woe again and again, but you are not sure how to stop yourself. As a result, that baggage keeps getting heavier to the point that sometimes you become paralyzed in your own sadness and memories. A few events can turn you into a bitter and unhappy person. That is not the way you are supposed to live your life. Especially at work, where you spend the majority of your life, ask yourself, do you want to be miserable eight to ten hours a day? Is that really living?

**You are meant for so much more happiness. Every day.**

What can you do to move forward and feel more free and joyful without all of that heavy baggage you are carrying around?

### 1. Ask yourself, "How do I want to live my life today?

Instead of making a to-do list, replace it with your "To Be" list. My friend and author, Starla J. King, talks about how having and following a To Be list is so much more rewarding than just checking off those chores every day. Write down how you want to feel and behave today—angry, tired, or sad? Or grateful, curious, and giving? When you look at it this way, the answer is a no-brainer, right?

## 2. Be bold and let it go.

At some point, we all become stuck in our routines, those known things that somehow give us comfort because we do them often and know what to expect. *Do one thing differently today.* You have heard me encourage you before to **Be Bold**. I have gotten so many comments on how just changing one little thing—like stopping yourself from complaining about the boss or the coffee, or being more patient with a co-worker or child who annoys you—can give you a new feeling of freedom and lightness. *Let go of those habits that no longer serve you.* Add some new ones that will recharge your energy. You will love the feeling.

## 3. Unpack your bags.

Take a little inventory of how much useless, emotional stuff you really have with you every day and night. Have a little notebook or use your mobile device to jot down the things that come up each day:

- What annoys you, sets you off, makes you sad or angry, or keeps you frozen from doing what you want?

- Is it that other people have so much more than you and you feel frustrated or left out?

- Are others asking too much and you can't say no and it makes you angry?

- Do you do things you don't want to and then resent it?

You get the picture. As you write the answers to these questions down, every day you will start to see a pattern. These loaded, emotional words that drain you will pop out. These are the ones you want to unpack.

**First be aware of how you are feeling and then choose to react differently,** in a more loving and nourishing manner toward both yourself and others. Pretty soon your bags will become so much lighter and filled with nothing but the "essentials" you need to move through your life more happily! Your new journey awaits you— starting today!

### *Just Be*

Most days we have to be somewhere, be doing something, or be someone we may not want to be. How many times do we just find a rock, perch ourselves, and allow our lives to take a time-out with nowhere to go and nothing to do?

On my morning walk the other day, this plump seagull was just standing around watching the water ebb and flow. I thought about how enriched our lives would be if we would just take even ten or fifteen minutes a day to drink in the world around us. To look up at the sky, or find a quiet spot like a church or museum. To sit on a bench in the park. To listen to the sound of laughter and children playing. You can feel what will bring you peace if you just surrender to life around you.

So, how will you make this happen? Make a small promise to yourself and say, "I MUST." Or better yet, put it right in the present with "I AM." For example, "I am getting up from my desk and looking at the sky. I am taking a quick walk to breathe in the air outside and clear my head." You know what to do. Make a little list of two or three things if you need to. The important part is to do it.

Find your own rock where you can sit down and just "be." I promise you will smile more today as you find little joys all around you. Your thoughts will be clearer, and you will be inspired or even inspire and bring joy to others. Now, that is a good day.

Ultimately, what I have found is that throughout our journey and all our pain, we have the choice to decide how we want to live. Now is the time to remove the disappointments that burden us. It is time to re-center around radical, complete honesty.

The truth is, no one is making you wear that heavy coat of suffering. You know how to unbutton it; you know how to throw it aside. In doing that, you will immediately experience a great lightening of your heart and your soul.

In taking charge of yourself, you will find a complete freedom.

What I have learned is that doing this is a forever action. Each and every day, we must wake up and decide how we want our life to continue, how we want to progress, and most importantly, how we want to feel.

So, when I wake up, I ask myself these simple questions:

- How do I decide to feel today?

- What can I do that is good and kind?

- Where and how can I feel joy in little moments?

- How can I take care of my whole self today—my spirit, mind, body, and soul?

*Have these questions helped me along my journey in staying mindful and intentional each day?* Yes.

*Do I do it every day?* Not quite, but I am working on it. Consistency is a practice, and something that must be trained daily.

### *What Fills Me Up?*

This is a question that has fueled my journey so far. What fills me up? What brings me joy when everything looks bleak? What centers me and realigns my priorities?

What I have learned is that it is the small things that fill me up the most. They are the things that are always there waiting for me when I need them. They are more powerful than the extravagances of life. They are simple, they are sweet, and they are my saving grace.

- *The sunrise when I can get myself up that early.*

- *My work—serving my clients. My professional family whom I help and who nourish me in return*

- *My prayers of love and gratitude.*

- *The clouds in the sky and the stars and the moon.*

- *Talking to my daughter each day.*

- *Traveling to new places and meeting new friends.*

- *Getting a new haircut or a fun new top.*

- *Dinner with friends.*

- *Beach weekends with my summer family.*

So, ask yourself—**What fills you up?**

What I have found is that anything that helps me stop and live in the moment brings me the most joy and healing; that is what gives me a new trajectory, a new path, and a new chance at hope.

While I wish I could tell you that these things have healed me, I know I'm not there yet. What I can tell you is that I have I have a plan—a plan to be aware of how I am feeling each day feeling each day—a plan that allows me to choose to strive for happiness each and every day. I have a plan that shows me the way toward the life I want to have, in spite of its challenges and the pain and the loss.

What's next for me is yet to be seen, but I know that it is a future I am in control of. I know we are not meant to live in pain or sorrow.

If you are wrestling as well with the pain of a loss, the pain of a life filled with disappointment, or a life that for whatever reason simply feels empty—know that you are not alone, and know that you are experiencing something that is simply a step on your journey. You have a well of power inside you, waiting for the moments when you need it most. You also have a team of angels around you ready to show you the way, ready to help you find what you are lacking in your life and bring you to a place of peace and serenity.

Now, all you have to do is ask for help.

### *Take Time Now to Reflect*

1. Look outside of yourself and share the best version of you with others. You never know how powerful your kindness is for others.

2. Laughter is not an option—it is essential for a joyful life.

3. Ask yourself EVERY day, "How do I decide to feel today?" You get to choose—stop giving away that power to someone else.

4. Write down at least 3–5 things that fill you up. Practice those wonderful, loving things to bring you joy.

# You Will Find Your Way to Joy

I want to thank you for allowing me the time and space to share my journey with you. It has been an important step on my way to healing, and now I want to return the gift to you.

You are not alone in this journey. Every day, know that you are surrounded by millions of others who are on a similar path, who are feeling similar pain, and who want deeply to share their insights and love—all in the effort of helping you heal.

We are a tribe. We are the only support we have for one another.

What I have learned most throughout my path to healing is that I cannot do this alone. I have so much power inside me, but I still cannot do this alone. There is no reason to suffer in silence.

Find your community, a teacher, a mentor or a coach, and build the team you need to heal.

We are here waiting for you. It's time to begin.

# Acknowledgements

Where to begin? All of my family, dearest friends, and teachers in my life have brought me love and teachings that have helped me become who I am today. I will list here, however, the women and men who have been my support and lifted me up and brought laughter to my life.

Of course, my beloved Harry. My daughter Sarah, who is my joy and rock, and who teaches me about life and fun and how to keep going when life becomes tough.

My Family of Cousins, the Cheri and the Lesko tribe, who are always there for me to get in trouble with! Joann, Erin, and the rest of the summer family—we are always ready to party and enjoy life.

Bryan Gregg for your courage.

My Greatest Teachers:

Lorin Beller Blake, coach, author, and my personal and business coach for many years, who has stuck by me and encouraged me to be better, no matter what.

John and Kathleen LaValle, dear friends for many years, renowned NLP Trainers and authors, who taught me to use my brain and that having fun needs to happen every day.

Paul Hartunian—a great teacher, friend, and mentor as I navigated my way through life changes.

Davidji—teacher, author, meditation master who, for the last ten years, has inspired me every day as I learn about Spirit and Soul and how there is so much more to life than what we see.

A special thanks to my mindset coach and chief cheerleader as I go through another Life Transition.

My clients—With love and gratitude to my amazing clients all over the world—I thank you for what you have taught me and for being open to learn and grow and create joy in your lives and businesses.

To my tribe of women—the true Troublemakers—I love each and every one of you. There is so much love, inspiration, and courage in this tribe (for many on this list have been through their own sorrows and challenges and come out strong and still loving life), and we all know how to have some great fun! In putting this list together, I am filled with gratitude that you are in my life!

Esther Hughes, Ann Zuckerman, Susan Best Jones, Eileen Galbraith, Linda Lovero Waterhouse, Katy DiBerbardo, Cathy Kurpiewski, Kate Falciani, Lisa Foley, Kathy Molyneaux, Kathy Cavallo, Lori Pace, Mel Bennett, Andi Parkhill, Pam Smith, Pat Horan, Rula Casey, Robyn Sweeney, Debbie Vincent, Leslie Vincent, Nancy Tausek, Madeleine Kineavy, Carol Strelic, Carol Walkner, Suzanne MacMurray, and the other truly gifted, loving healers at the Center for Conscious Caregiving, Suzanne Arden, Dhana Thoulson, Deborah Fell, Linda Sinsical, Jayme Huleatt, Mary Polese, Mary Tobin, Rebecca Cohen, Jill Searing and Christine Gallagher.

If I have overlooked anyone, I know there are more of you, I truly am sorry. Know you are in my heart.

A special thank you to Starla J. King for being my friend and first writing teacher and one of the most creative people I have ever known. Starla has given me the cover photo—besides being a gifted writer, she is an incredible photographer. Thank you, Starla!

Many thanks to Ally Nathaniel, AN Better Publishing for her extreme patience and support on this project. My stops and starts really tested her, I am sure, but she has shown extreme professionalism and support all along the way. Thank you, Ally. I am honored to know and work with you.

A very special appreciation to Brett Dameron, an extremely talented actor and movie producer, who helped me so much in the writing of this book—his creativity and guidance were with me all along the way. Thank you from my heart.

Extra gratitutde to my extraordinary photographer, who took the photos on the Author page and back cover....Patty D. Marchesi at www.pattydphotography.com. You always make it fun!

Special thanks to Anita Jones, Another Jones Graphics, for her book design expertise and to Sharon Castlen, Integrated Book Marketing, for her vision of the book and how to market it to those who will benefit.

# Book Club Study Questions

### Chapter One
1. When were the times in your life that you felt you played small?
2. Why do you think that happened?
3. Do you know what you need to stop playing small now?
4. What does one Tiny Moment of Joy you create do to make you smile and laugh, and make your heart sing—if only for a few minutes?

### Chapter Two
1. What behaviors or feelings do you still have now that are holding you back?
2. What do you need—internal or external—to start to let go of what no longer serves you?
3. What is one Tiny Moment of Joy you can create to make you smile and laugh, and make your heart sing—if only for a few minutes?

### Chapter Three
1. Do you believe you are capable of creating your own magic? If not, why do you think that is?
2. Do you believe others contribute more to the magic in your life? In what ways?
3. What is your limiting belief that is getting in the way of creating more magic in your life?
4. What is one Tiny Moment of Joy you will create to make more magic in your life?

## *Chapter Four*

1. What are your 2–3 most powerful self-limiting beliefs? Be honest about this. For example—I'm too old; I don't have the right education, I don't have the energy/smarts/freedom to get my dream job/partner, etc.
2. What is the one thing for each of these beliefs that I can do right now to let them go?
3. What support do I need to let them go?
4. In what ways am I creative?
5. How can I give myself permission and allow myself to create the life I want?

## *Chapter Five*

1. In what ways do you make your life harder than it needs to be?
2. What makes you laugh? What can you practice every day to laugh more?
3. How can you add laughter or find some fun in the "atomic bombs" that drop into your life?

## *Chapter Six*

1. What do you love best about the real world you are in?
2. What do you like least about your real world?
3. Take time now to acknowledge the Wild Woman, the authentic you. How would you describe that person?
4. What is holding you back?

## *Chapter Seven*

1. What were the times in your life when you said "Why Not," and reflecting back, they turned out to be some of the best decisions you ever made?
2. How did letting loose and going after what you wanted make you feel? It's very important to describe this—don't just say "fine" or "good." Dig in and remember what it really felt like— if it made you feel energized, made you smile, feel like you were fully alive, etc.

3. What did you learn from this letting go?
4. What stops you now from letting go?
5. What are one or two things you can do to go for "Why Not"?
6. Are there relationships you need to repair and find forgiveness? Sometimes it is not possible, but how can you forgive yourself and move forward?

## Chapter Eight
1. When is it time for you to let go; to accept and move on?
2. What are you holding on to in your life that is dragging you down? What delays you from making decisions that will bring you joy?
3. What values do you hold most dear in your life that you have hidden and need to honor now, that will allow you to move forward?

## Chapter Nine
1. What were the times in your life when you ignored your instincts?
2. What were the consequences of that?
3. How can you be better at listening to your inner voice that will guide you to better decisions? What do you need?

## Chapter Ten
1. What were the times in your life when your Wild Woman took over and you stood up for what you believed and needed?
2. How did that feel? (Again, be very descriptive.)
3. How can you cultivate that power within you? What do you need?
4. Be aware of your own obstacles. What are they in each of the categories above?

## Chapter Eleven
1. What were (or what are now) the times in your life when you feel you were/are not heard?
2. How does it make you feel when you're overlooked?

3. What do you think is the root cause of this? Be brutally honest—is it how you come across? Are you being overrun in a man's world?
4. What are one or two things you can do to overcome this?

## Chapter Twelve

1. How do you normally deal with your emotional or spiritual pain? Write this down.
2. What is effective?
3. What is not effective?
4. What can you do to react to this pain in a different way— one that you see as a growth opportunity?

## Chapter Thirteen

1. How can you open yourself up for more joy? Write down everything you can think of so that opportunities for happiness come your way and you are ready to receive them.

## Chapter Fourteen

1. What do you want your legacy to be? This is one of the most important questions you can ask yourself. Put aside some real quiet time to answer this.
2. How do you describe yourself now? Is there a gap?
3. How do you want others to describe you? What do you want them to say about you now and at the end of your life?

## Chapter Fifteen

1. Who are the angels in your life?
2. Do you reach out to them and thank them in whatever way is best?
3. Write down what you want your anchors to be (or what they already are) to help you in the hard times.
4. What are two things that will help you to empower yourself and choose joy?

### Chapter Sixteen

1. Write a "To Be" list for yourself. How do you want to think, feel, and be each day?
2. What are the top priorities in your life now?
3. Given the state of our world, what do you do differently?
4. Do you have a need to be perfect? If so, identify when those times are and how to respond differently.

### Chapter Seventeen

1. What worries do you have, if any, about getting older (no matter what your age is)?
2. What do you want to do that you have not already done? Be specific here.
3. What are your ideas on how to make that happen?

### Chapter Eighteen

1. How do you come across to others when you are not your best self? How do others see you?
2. What can you do to be more aware of the reactions of others—of how to be mindful that this is not just about you?
3. What are three "little joys" you can do for yourself every day?
4. What do you need to do to make a commitment to these changes?

### Chapter Nineteen

1. Look outside of yourself and share the best version of you with others. You never know how powerful your kindness is for others.
2. Laughter is not an option—it is essential for a joyful life.
3. Ask yourself EVERY day, "How do I decide to feel today?" You get to choose—stop giving away that power to someone else.
4. Write down at least 3–5 things that fill you up. Practice those wonderful, loving things that bring you joy.

# A Special Thank-You

Congratulations! You have decided to show yourself a little love, and I want to acknowledge you joining me on this journey. As a thank you for **reading** this book, I want to give you something today.

### The Love Yourself Scorecard

I have developed this enlightening little self-assessment that helps you to identify where you are in your self-love. We are happy you are here, and I am gifting you the "Love Yourself Scorecard©". The discovery process about you awaits when you take this survey. This Love Yourself Scorecard, used exclusively in my programs, will give you information and a method to get you started on knowing so much more about yourself. This will help you move toward finding what you really love to do—Live with Joy.

To download YOUR scorecard, go to www.ticwl.com and scroll down to the bottom of the page.

# Join Us for More

**Visit our website** for upcoming events, helpful articles for your journey and an opportunity to connect with us for a community and support!

### The International Center for Women's Leadership
### https://ticwl.com

If you would like to be informed about noteworthy articles, videos, programs, and conferences just for women, plus upcoming events at the International Center for Women, please go to https://ticwl.com/contact/ and join us (no charge ever for this service). We only provide **relevant and noteworthy information** on a periodic basis, and will never give your email or other data to anyone else. That is our promise.

# Resources

These books are here to help you continue on your journey. There are additional websites and organizations on the website, www.ticwl.com.

Brown, Brené. *Daring Greatly How the Courage to Be Vulnerable Transforms the Way We Live, Love, Parent, and Lead.* Avery: 2012

Durst, Dr. Michael G. *Napkin Notes: On the Art of Living Responsibly.* Life Foundation: 2010.

Dyer, Dr. Wayne. *The Power of Intention.* Hay House: 2005.

Estés, Clarissa Pinkola. *Women Who Run with the Wolves.* Ballantine Books: (multiple editions) 1996.

Forleo. Marie. *Everything is Figuroutable.* Penguin Publishing Group: 2019.

Gilbert, Elizabeth. *Big Magic: Creative Living Beyond Fear.* Riverhead Books: 2015.

Ruiz, Miguel. *The Four Agreements: A Practical Guide to Personal Freedom.* Amber-Allen Publishing: 2001.

Trent, Dr. Terrerai. *The Awakened Woman: Remembering & Reigniting Our Sacred Dreams.* Atria/Enliven Books: 2017.

Walker, Alice. *The Color Purple.* Penguin Books: 2019.

# About the Author, Speaker, and The International Center for Women's Leadership

Marybeth Gregg is the President and Founder of the International Center for Women's Leadership. Throughout her 30+ year career, she has worked in human development for several global corporations, in addition to her extensive individual coaching work with clients in the business and not-for-profit arena. In 2012, Marybeth founded The International Center for Women, now known as the International Center for Women's Leadership. This woman-owned-and-operated organization is dedicated to supporting women during personal life changes, mid-life journeys, partnership transition, retirement, or simply for women who are in search of a more meaningful and fulfilling life.

Drawing on her own personal losses, career changes, life challenges and victories, Marybeth Gregg brings a unique combination of empathy and experience to her work with women who need, and are ready, to take charge of their own lives.

Marybeth speaks in-person and virtually at conferences, workshops, retreats, small groups and corporate events with a focus on being a leader in your own life and taking charge to create your own plan to realized your dreams.

**For more information about Marybeth, for media interviews or to schedule appointments for consulting work and speaking, contact Marybeth and The Center at:**

Website: www.ticwl.com   Direct email: marybeth@ticwl.com

# Take Charge and Create the Plan to Realize Your Dreams — The Time for You is Now.

CPSIA information can be obtained
at www.ICGtesting.com
Printed in the USA
JSHW020018070322
23498JS00002B/8